CULTURE SMART!
CHINA

Kathy Flower

ISBN 978 1 85733 854 6
This book is also available as an e-book: eISBN 978 1 85733 855 3

British Library Cataloguing in Publication Data
A CIP catalogue entry for this book is available from the British Library

First published in Great Britain
by Kuperard, an imprint of Bravo Ltd
59 Hutton Grove, London N12 8DS
Tel: +44 (0) 20 8446 2440 Fax: +44 (0) 20 8446 2441
www.culturesmart.co.uk
Inquiries: sales@kuperard.co.uk

Series Editor Geoffrey Chesler
Design Bobby Birchall

Printed in Malaysia

About the Author

KATHY FLOWER has worked in the UK and China as a BBC radio producer, TV presenter, scriptwriter, teacher, and trainer. She spent four years with the British Council in Paris, and was copresenter of an English-language teaching series on French TV. This led her to Beijing, where she copresented China's first major English-language teaching series, "Follow Me," on Chinese TV. She became known to hundreds of millions of enthusiastic Chinese viewers as "Fay-lau-ah *laoshi*," or "Teacher Flower." Back in London she joined BBC World Service Radio. Kathy has returned to China many times to work and travel. She now teaches international students, including many young Chinese enrolled at British universities, and lives in Hampshire and southern France.

The Culture Smart! series is continuing to expand.
For further information and latest titles visit
www.culturesmart.co.uk

The publishers would like to thank **CultureSmart!**Consulting for its help in researching and developing the concept for this series.

CultureSmart!Consulting creates tailor-made seminars and consultancy programs to meet a wide range of corporate, public-sector, and individual needs. Whether delivering courses on multicultural team building in the USA, preparing Chinese engineers for a posting in Europe, training call-center staff in India, or raising the awareness of police forces to the needs of diverse ethnic communities, it provides essential, practical, and powerful skills worldwide to an increasingly international workforce.

For details, visit www.culturesmartconsulting.com

CultureSmart!Consulting and **CultureSmart!** guides have both contributed to and featured regularly in the weekly travel program "Fast Track" on BBC World TV.

contents

contents

Map of China

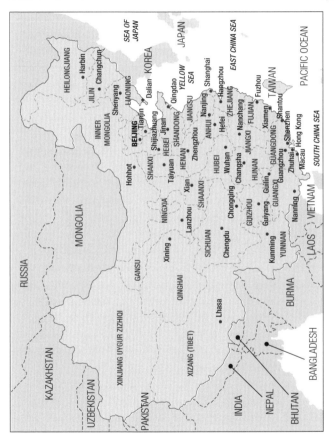

introduction

Since 1979, when Premier Deng Xiao Peng declared China open for business, millions of its citizens have been lifted out of poverty and given the chance to control their own destinies. Initially China achieved its spectacular growth by "making and selling things we want at prices we can afford," as *The Economist* put it; three decades on, it is a major player on the global stage, courted by governments worldwide.

Having become rich, new China has made peace with its past. Old China's once derelict temples and palaces have been restored to vibrant life and draw huge crowds, while new China's futuristic cities are on a par with Tokyo, London, or New York.

Behind these economic miracles lie the Chinese people, 1.4 billion individuals, each one part of a family unit. Where Western family sagas focus on illicit love affairs and property, Chinese family sagas offer a guide to the country's turbulent history. Perhaps most famous is Jung Chang's bestselling autobiography, *Wild Swans: Three Daughters of China*. The first daughter was Yu Fang, Jung Chang's grandmother; as a small child her feet were bound and then she was sold to a warlord as one of his concubines. Her daughter by him was to become Jung Chang's mother, Bao Qin, a founder member of China's Communist Party. Jung Chang, born in 1952, at first had a privileged childhood; but when the orchestrated chaos of Mao Zedong's Cultural Revolution began in the 1960s, her parents were denounced and tortured. Eventually Jung Chang gained a scholarship to England and left for good. Nowadays, generations of daughters (and sons) of China are free to study abroad, to travel, and to work toward their own dreams. But competition is fierce in today's market oriented China, and traditional beliefs in the importance of hard work, a good education, and a supportive family are stronger than ever.

China's outward-looking economic agenda is very recent. In the past, its size meant it did not need to engage with anyone outside its borders. China saw itself as the center of the world; peoples on the periphery were considered barbarians, to be graciously received by the Emperor and then dismissed. From the sixteenth century onward, Europeans who tried to establish links with China were equally politely rebuffed.

After the Communist takeover in 1949, China remained closed to the West. Not until 1971 could US envoy Henry Kissinger go secretly to Beijing to meet Mao, followed in 1972 by President Nixon himself. But after Mao's death in 1976, Deng Xiaoping opened China's doors, putting it on the path to prosperity and changing it, and the world, in the process. The Chinese you will meet in this fascinating country are well educated, warm, knowledgeable about world affairs, and keen to talk about everything under the sun. This book should help you to be a "good guest," whether you are there for work, pleasure, or both.

Key Facts

Official Name	The People's Republic of China (PRC); in Mandarin, *Zhonghua Renmin Gonghe Guo*	The island of Taiwan, which has its own government, is called the ROC (Republic of China).
Capital City	Beijing (Peking) *Bei* = north *jing* = capital	"Peking" is the old Wade–Giles form of transliterating the city's name.
Main Cities	Chongqing (Chungking), Shenyang (Mukden), Wuhan, Nanjing (Nanking), Harbin	Major ports: Tianjin (Tientsin), Shanghai, Qingdao (Tsingtao), Guangzhou (Canton)
Area	3,695,500 sq. miles (9,571,300 sq. km)	The third largest country in the world
Terrain	Mountains, deserts, and arid basins in the north and northwest. Mountainous in the south. Rolling hills and plains in the east.	Two-thirds mountain or desert. The low-lying east is irrigated by the rivers Huang He (Yellow River), Chang Jiang (Yangtze Kiang), and Xi Jiang (Si Kiang).
Climate	Temperatures vary greatly in the arid north and west, with hot summers and very cold dry winters.	The south and east are warm and humid, with rainfall all year-round.
Population	The world's most populous country: 1.4 billion est. (UN figures, 2014)	Roughly one in four people in the world live in China.
Population Density	Shanghai has 7,000 people per sq. mile; Beijing 1,927 per sq. mile; Tibet, only 5 people per sq. mile.	Most people live in the eastern central region, on the fertile flood plains and the eastern coastal region.

Urban/Rural Divide	The World Bank estimated that about 54% of China's population live and work in cities. Migrant workers from the countryside have powered the Chinese economy for three decades.	The household registration system (*hukou*) means that rural-born workers may live in cities for years, but still belong to their area of origin. They have been treated as second-class citizens, but are now claiming equality with city dwellers.
Ethnic Makeup	Roughly 92% are Han Chinese; the rest are made up of 55 officially recognized "national minorities."	Minorities are small in number, but concentrated in border regions, thus politically important.
Age Structure	0–14 years: 17.2%; 15–64 years: 73.4% (2012); 65 and over: 9.4% (UN, 2012). China's one child policy has led to fewer young people than in most developing countries.	Health care has improved and the population is getting older: by 2020, 11.8% of the population will be over 65.
Life Expectancy	Men: 74 ; Women: 77 (WHO, 2015). The worldwide average is 68 for men, 73 for women.	Prior to 1949, historians say that average life expectancy was about 35 years.
Adult Literacy Rate	96.4% (UNESCO, 2015). Illiteracy more common among much older people, ethnic minorities, and in rural areas due to poor schooling.	Even when learning to read at school, it is easy to forget Chinese characters if they are not used every day; this is less of a problem with alphabets.

Languages	Mandarin (official), Cantonese, Wu, and others. All share the same script, though Taiwan and Hong Kong use traditional Chinese characters; the mainland uses simplified ones.	Other minority languages exist such as Tibetan, and more in the southwest, where the minorities mostly live.
Religion	Officially atheist. Traditionally Daoist, Confucian, and Buddhist. Minority religious groups: Muslim, Christians.	Christianity and Buddhism are growing in popularity. The Communist Party is cautiously tolerant of organized religion.
Government	Ruled by the Communist Party since 1949.	There are other parties, but no general elections on the Western model.
Economy	From 1979 China moved away from a Soviet-style centrally planned economy to a free market one, and now accounts for 17% of global economic activity. Wages in China are rising. Automation is replacing people.	
Currency	Renminbi, "people's money." Also known as the yuan (dollar). 1 renminbi/yuan = 10 jiao = 100 fen. There are 1, 5, 10, 20, 50, and 100 yuan notes.	In transition from a "soft" to a "hard" currency. The Renminbi was devalued in August 2015. It is not yet freely convertible.
Resources	Natural resources, such as gasoline, natural gas, coal, uranium; mineral resources incl. iron, manganese, and zinc; non-metallic mineral resources incl. graphite, phosphorus, and sulfur.	Deforestation in the southwest is being tackled by replanting. According to the UN FAO about 22% of China is covered by forest; about 5.6% of this is "primary forest", the most bio-diverse kind.

Agriculture	No longer self-sufficient in food, China imports food such as meat, wheat, and dairy products.	Most milk is now imported from New Zealand and food safety has become a major concern.
Growth Rate	From 1989 to 2015, GDP grew by nearly 10%. Growth in 2015 was 6.9%.	
Main Exports	Electronic equipment, machines, engines, pumps, furniture, lighting, signs, clothing, medical, technical equipment, plastics, vehicles. China is the largest export economy in the world (2014). It is also the second-largest importer in the world.	
Electricity	220 volts, 50 Hz	Wall sockets have three connectors. Adaptors needed.
Media: Traditional	State-controlled and subject to censorship. *Renmin Ribao* (*People's Daily*) is the Party newspaper. Chinese Central TV (CCTV) is the state broadcaster.	There are about 3,000 regional TV and radio stations, and increasing numbers of foreign broadcasters.
Media: English Language	CCTV broadcasts in English and other foreign languages. There is an active (mostly state-run) English-language press. *China Daily* is published six days a week, with a *Business Weekly* on Sunday. There are also English-language online sites on many topics.	
Internet Domain	.cn The main search engine is Baidu.	The government monitors Internet use and employs "microblog monitors."
TV/DVDs	Pal system used. Most households have TV.	
Telephone	International country code: 00 86	
Time Difference	GMT + 8 hrs	Although China extends across five time zones, Beijing time is used.

chapter one

LAND & PEOPLE

"*For millennia . . . Chinese civilization stretched over an area larger than any European state. Chinese language and culture . . . extended to every known terrain: steppes and pine forests in the north, shading into Siberia, tropical jungles and terraced rice farms in the south; from the coast with its canals, ports, and fishing villages, to the stark deserts of Central Asia and the ice capped peaks of the Himalayan frontier.*"

Henry Kissinger, *On China,* 2011

TERRAIN AND CLIMATE

China has a total landmass of 3.7 million square miles (9.6 million sq. km), next in size only to Russia and Canada. At its maximum, it measures approximately 3,100 miles (5,000 km) north–south, and 3,230 miles (5,200 km) east–west. Its land border is 14,168 miles (22,800 km) long. Apart from the mainland, there are more than 5,400 islands, some just bare rocks that only appear at low tide. Technically speaking, it encompasses five time zones from the east coast across to the Russian border in the west.

Most rivers flow west to east into the Pacific Ocean. The Yangtze River (Chang Jiang) is the longest at 3,915 miles (6,300 km)—and third longest in the

world after the Nile and the Amazon—followed
by the Yellow River (Huang He) at 3,395 miles
(5,464 km), the birthplace of Chinese civilization.
However, in recent years, the Yellow River has been
shortened by several hundred miles for months on
end, due to having dried up near its delta.

China is a land of extremes, and temperatures vary
widely. In northern China, summers are hot and short,
winters long and cold. The humidity in the north in
summer is unpleasant—around 60–70 percent—and
the lack of moisture in the winter, when humidity
falls to about 2 percent, is even worse, as are the dust
storms caused by sand blowing in from the Gobi
Desert.

To the north of the capital, Beijing, lie the vast
empty grasslands of the Inner Mongolian Plateau.
Mongolia is swept by winds from Siberia and is bitterly
cold in winter, sometimes as low as minus 35°C
(-31°F), but with fine, sunny days. The northeastern
Mongolian town of Harbin is famous for its annual
winter display of huge sculptures made of ice blocks,

taken from the Songhua River, and lit from inside by colored lanterns; starting around January 5, the festival lasts for about a month, until its sculptures start to melt away with the coming of spring. The south of China is more temperate, and in recent years northerners have started retiring there to enjoy the milder climate.

China is a country of superlatives. The world's highest mountain, Mount Everest (Zhumulangma Feng in Chinese), forms China's western border with Nepal and India. It is part of the Himalayan range of mountains, forty of whose peaks rise to over 22,900 feet (7,000 m). In the northwest is the Tarim Basin, the largest inland basin in the world. To the east of the Tarim Basin is the low-lying Turpan depression, called the "Oasis of Fire," the hottest place in China, with temperatures of up to 120°F (49°C) in summer. Xinjiang, where an ethnic minority called the Uigurs live, is also home to the Taklamakan, the largest desert in China. The oasis towns of the vast empty desert areas were used for two thousand years as stopovers on the Silk Route—from the time of the Romans, caravans of camels would carry silk to the West. Salt from China's largest salt lake, Lop Nur, also went this way. Whoever controlled the oases could tax this traffic, so despite its arid deserts, Xinjiang was an attractive prize.

In the south, vegetation remains green all year-round. The coastal regions are warm and humid, with four distinct seasons. The south and southwest of China have a much more agreeable climate, with lush green vegetation and beautiful wooded mountains wreathed in mists. The southwest is the home of bamboo forests and the panda; also of many plants familiar in the West, such as rhododendrons, some of which were brought over to Europe by nineteenth-century botanists.

Only about 20 percent of the terrain is suitable for agriculture. The majority of the Han population has for centuries lived mainly on the fertile floodplains

at the lower reaches of the Yellow River and the Yangtze River. These two rivers deposit silt, which makes the flood plain the richest agricultural area in China. This is where the main cities have grown up, along with key industries. So much of China is uninhabitable that around 90 percent of the people, mainly Han Chinese, are squeezed into about half of the area. The government has tried to resettle people in more sparsely populated areas, such as Tibet and Xinjiang, but the Han do not really want to live there and the locals are not keen to have them.

Nowadays China's ambitions are much more futuristic: they are creating huge new cities, and then filling them with people. There are nearly 600 more cities now than when the Communists took over in 1949. Some have been labelled "ghost towns," because the buildings stand empty, seemingly for years, waiting for the population to arrive; but though building a new city is quite quick, putting in place the infrastructure and services for anything up to

30 million people takes time. The Chinese traditionally take a long-term view of things, and these new cities, for all their eerie emptiness, are part of that vision.

HAN CHINESE AND MINORITY NATIONALITIES

Ninety-two percent of the population of China are of the Han race, or what the West calls Chinese. Minority nationalities generally live in the northwestern and southwestern extremities of the country. Fifty-five minority nationalities are officially recognized, totalling just over 100 million people. They have their own customs, languages, dress, and religions. Many in the northwest, near the borders with Pakistan, Afghanistan, India, and Russia, follow Islam. Tibetans, Mongolians, Lobas, Moinbas, Tus, and Yugurs are Lamaists. The Dai, Blang, and Deang people are Buddhists, while many of the Miao, Yao, and Yi people are Christian. Official attitudes toward them are a complex mixture of tolerance and control.

Mandarin is promoted as the official language and all minority peoples learn it. The government has also helped to create written languages for ten minority nationalities, including the Zhuang, Bouyei, Miao, Dong, Hani, and Li, which prior to 1949 had only spoken languages. The minority nationalities have a geopolitical importance far beyond their numbers because of the strategic territories they occupy along China's sparsely populated and porous frontiers; partly due to this, they were exempted from the One Child policy (see page 35).

A BRIEF HISTORY

The fertile floodplains of the Yellow River were the cradle of Chinese civilization. Thousands of years ago the Chinese were already weaving silk, carving jade, casting bronze, growing wheat, millet, and rice, and recording events in a written language. The crossbow, used in Europe in the Middle Ages, was invented in China some fifteen centuries earlier. A thousand years before the Industrial Revolution in Britain, China already had coke ovens and steel blast furnaces. Chinese art, science, architecture, language, literature, and philosophy continue to be studied and admired around the world.

The Chinese will tell you, with pride, of their five thousand years of history, but in fact it goes back even further. Archaeologists have found evidence of Neolithic sites dating from before 5000 BCE. The earliest-known dynasty was the Xia, which ruled about 1994–1523 BCE. By the time of the Shang (or Yin) dynasty, which flourished in the Yellow River valley in 1523–1027 BCE, a sophisticated culture had developed, with advanced bronze-manufacturing, a written language, and the first Chinese calendar.

The Zhou and the Mandate of Heaven

The last Shang ruler was a tyrant who was overthrown by the founders of the Zhou (or Chou) dynasty (1027–255 BCE). This period saw the introduction of money, iron, written laws, and the ethical philosophy of Confucianism, and gave birth to the idea of the "Mandate of Heaven"(*Tien Ming*), in which Heaven gives wise rulers a mandate to rule, but takes it away from corrupt ones. The Emperor became known as

the "Son of Heaven," a concept that still had potency right up until Mao Zedong's death in 1976. Later, the "Mandate of Heaven" incorporated the Daoist belief that Heaven sends natural disasters such as earthquakes and floods to show its disapproval of bad rulers.

During the Zhou period the Chinese people's sense of their unique identity and cultural superiority developed. The name *Zhong Guo*, or "Middle Kingdom," was coined to describe the central importance of China: anyone outside it was considered to be a barbarian. *Zhong Guo* is still the name used by the Chinese today to refer to modern China; foreigners are referred to as *waiguoren*, or "outside country people."

The Warring States Period (c. 500–221 BCE)
Civil war followed the Zhou dynasty's reign, and the Zhou empire broke up into small kingdoms. The philosopher Confucius declared that the Zhou empire had been a golden age, and for centuries afterward

the Chinese looked back on it as an idealized time.
Eventually, the Qin (pronounced "Chin") dynasty
defeated its rivals and united the warring feudal
states into a single empire.

The Qin Dynasty (221–207 BCE)
The Qin introduced centralized government, standard
weights and measures, writing systems, and money,
and built a network of roads that joined the capital
(near modern-day Xi'an) to the distant outposts of the
empire. The first Qin Emperor, Qin Shi Huang, used
thousands of slaves to continue the building of the
Great Wall of China, designed to keep out the "Mongol
hordes." Much of the original Great Wall has collapsed
now, its stones carted off to build houses for the
locals—whose ancestors helped to build the original
wall. The parts that are still standing have been heavily
restored and are visited by millions every year.

Qin Shi Huang was buried in Chang'an (today
Xi'an). With him were buried the now world-famous

terracotta army of around 8,000 life size-soldiers, 130 chariots, and 670 horses, who stand guard over him; using clay figures brought to an end the barbaric tradition of burying real people alive to escort the Emperor's body into the next world.

The Han Dynasty (206 BCE–9 CE and 25–220 CE)
 The Han dynasty saw the Chinese empire expand into central Asia, and the growth of centralized rule. The position of the Emperor changed from that of sole and absolute ruler to one in which power was delegated to a highly developed civil service. A complicated examination system, based on the candidates' knowledge of Confucianism, was set up to select people to work as bureaucrats; it lasted more or less unchanged for two thousand years. Ever since, the Chinese people have referred to themselves as the *Han; Hanyu* is the Chinese language, and *Hanzi* is the name for Chinese characters.

The Sui Dynasty (581–618)
External rebellions and internal feuding eventually destroyed the Han and the empire split into three

competing kingdoms, resulting in the eventual victory of the Wei over the Chou and Wu. Confucianism was superseded by Buddhism, introduced from India, and by Daoism; and "barbarian" (known in the West as the Hun) invasions started in the north. The Sui dynasty then reunified China, halted the march of the Huns, and strengthened the Great Wall.

The Tang Dynasty (618–906)

The Sui were soon replaced by the Tang. This was a golden age for China. The Tang capital was in modern day Xi'an. Then called Chang'an, it was one of the world's greatest cities, rivaling Rome and Constantinople, with a population of one million and a society with many modern features such as commerce, tax collection, civil administration, tolerance of different religions,

and a thriving culture. The Tang era is famous for its poetry and ceramics. The Tang continued the creation of canals linking different parts of the empire, and built inns for traveling officials, merchants, and pilgrims to break their journeys. There was more contact with foreigners than at any other time until the late twentieth century. The Tang empire disintegrated into the "Five Dynasties and Ten Kingdoms," amid war and economic decline.

The Song Dynasty (960–1279)
Under the Song, China was unified again and order restored. This was a period of calm and creativity. However the frontiers were neglected and Mongol incursions began. Despite the Middle Kingdom's attempts to seal itself off from the outside world, foreigners continued to find their way in, as invaders, ambassadors, or merchants. The most famous traveler of all, Venetian merchant and explorer Marco Polo, visited China from 1275 to 1292. On his return to Venice he wrote the first eyewitness account of China, describing its wealthy cities, paper money, methods of salt production, and the burning of coal to create heat. His book inspired others such as Christopher Columbus to want to travel to China and a version of it has been in print ever since.

Some Chinese "Firsts"
The Chinese are proud of their "Four Great Inventions": papermaking, the compass, gunpowder, and printing. Engraved woodblock printing on paper and silk was invented in the seventh century; the world's oldest surviving printed book is a Chinese Buddhist text printed in 868 CE. Another Chinese first was the invention of moveable type in the eleventh century.

The Yuan Dynasty (1260–1368)

By the time of Marco Polo's arrival in China, the Mongols had poured across the Gobi Desert on their horses, undeterred by the Great Wall. They made Beijing their capital and Kublai Khan became the first emperor of the foreign Yuan dynasty—the first non-native emperor to conquer all of China. The Yuan were ruthless but efficient rulers; they improved the roads leading into China and Russia, promoted trade, and even set up a famine relief system.

The Ming Dynasty (1368–1644)

The Yuan were driven out, to be replaced by the first emperor of the native Han Chinese Ming dynasty, Zhu Yuanzhang, a man of poor peasant stock. Famine, natural disasters, hyperinflation, and corruption brought Ming rule to an end, hastened by an earthquake in 1556 that is thought to have killed 830,000 people. This sign that the emperor had lost the Mandate of Heaven strengthened his enemies; echoes of this belief were heard when the Tangshan earthquake of July 1976 killed about 240,000 people, just three months before Mao died.

The First Europeans Arrive

In 1516, two hundred and forty-one years after Marco Polo, Portuguese ships arrived off the coast of China. Portugal in the sixteenth century was a great trading nation with imperial ambitions, and the Portuguese were allowed to set up a trading post in Macau, to be followed by the British, Dutch, and Spanish. In 1582 an Italian Jesuit priest named Matteo Ricci arrived in Macau, learned Chinese, and then settled in Zhaoqing at the invitation of the governor, who had heard of Ricci's knowledge of mathematics and cartography. Ricci made the first European-style world map in Chinese; he also compiled a Portuguese–Chinese dictionary. Six copies of the original map on rice paper, made in 1602, still survive and there is a plaque commemorating Ricci in Zhaoqing.

The Qing Dynasty (1644–1912)

The Ming were succeeded by another non-Chinese dynasty, the Qing, nomads from Manchuria who, like all the other foreign rulers, soon assimilated into Chinese culture. The Qing government kept the Europeans as far away as possible, making them stay in Canton (now Guangzhou). But this did not prevent the start of a trade that was to become a byword for Western imperialism: the sale by the British of Indian-grown opium to the Chinese.

Opium had been used for centuries for pain relief, as an antidepressant, and to kill hunger pains. People were well aware of the risk of addiction, but nonetheless opium remained legal in Europe and the USA as late as the 1920s.

The Opium Wars

In exchange for selling opium the British were at last getting all the Chinese tea, silk, and porcelain they craved. But the numbers of addicts were growing rapidly and the Chinese Emperor tried to ban the trade in 1800; his decree was ignored. The trade continued unchecked until 1839, when the Chinese seized and burned 20,000 chests of opium. So began the first of the notorious Opium Wars (1839–42), with the British attacking Canton, forcing China to cede Hong Kong and to open five ports to European trade. There were to be more of these wars in the nineteenth century, fought by the British with support from the Russians, French, and Americans—and understandably influencing the Chinese view of Westerners as "foreign devils" for the next hundred years.

By 1860 the West had won huge concessions: foreigners could settle in many different parts of China, were exempt from Chinese laws, and the Chinese were forced to pay large war indemnities. As the nineteenth century drew to a close, the Throne of Heaven was occupied by the four-year-old Emperor, Kuang Hsu; but real power lay in the hands of his aunt, the

Dowager Empress, Tzu Hsi. Rather than bring China into the Industrial Age, she presided over its total disintegration.

The Boxer Rebellion

Worse was to come. The Dowager Empress raised taxes and added to the misery of the peasantry. War, floods, famine, and drought plagued the last years of the dying century, with the foreign powers profiting at China's expense. Peasant anger erupted in the Boxer Rebellion.

The anti-Western Society of the Harmonious Fist, known as the Boxers, was born in Shangdong province and nurtured by the weakened Qing government, who saw their popularity with the peasantry as a chance to chase foreigners out of China. The Boxers massacred foreign missionaries and Chinese Christians, destroyed churches and railway lines, and, in 1900, marched to Beijing and attacked the foreign compounds.

Rapid intervention by foreign troops meant that the Boxers lost this battle, but secret societies were springing up all over China, aimed at toppling the Qing dynasty and getting rid of the foreigners. In 1905 Dr. Sun Yat-sen, still revered today as the father of modern China, became the leader of one of these

revolutionary groups, the Guomindang (National People's Party), and events started to move fast. The Dowager Empress died in 1908, as did Kuang Hsu, and the two-year-old Pu Yi came to the throne—later immortalized in Bertolucci's memorable film *The Last Emperor* (1987). The little boy's reign was brief. Revolution broke out again in 1911. The Qing government acknowledged defeat and in 1912 Sun Yat-sen proclaimed the Republic of China.

Warlords, Nationalists, and Communists
After the abdication of the infant emperor, General Yuan Shihkai became dictator. On his death in 1916, central government collapsed and warlords ruled over small local fiefdoms. Extreme poverty and lawlessness were rife. In 1921 Dr.
Sun Yat-sen was elected President of the nominal National Government; the same year saw the founding of the Chinese Communist Party, which had strong links with the new Soviet regime in neighboring Russia. From 1923 the Communists

worked with the Guomindang to reunite China and gradually won the support of the Chinese peasants. But when Sun Yat-sen died in 1925, the new leader of the Guomindang, Chiang Kai-shek, declared war on the Communists.

Civil war began in 1926 and living conditions for the poor, already bad, deteriorated even further. American journalist Edgar Snow and other contemporary writers described in shocking detail how children worked in factories for twelve hours a day, hundreds starved to death on the streets, and how every night carts trundled through the cities, gathering up corpses as though they were so much rubbish. While the Communists and the Guomindang were fighting each other for control of China, the Japanese overran Manchuria

in 1932, set up the puppet state of Manchukuo, and in 1937 they attacked Shanghai. During the Second World War the various political groups united against the Japanese invaders, but from 1941 Chiang Kai-shek received help from the USA and Britain, which was to poison relations with Mao for many years afterward.

The Long March
In 1934–5 the Communists undertook the "Long March" from southeast to northwest China to escape encirclement by the Guomindang. Open civil war resumed in 1946, and in 1949 the Red Army led by Mao Zedong defeated the Nationalists at Nanjing. Chiang Kai-shek fled to the island of Formosa (now Taiwan), taking with him the entire gold reserves of

his impoverished country. On October 1, 1949—now
National Day and a public holiday—Mao Zedong
declared the People's Republic of China a reality.

The People's Republic

For a while daily life improved for most Chinese, and
some look back on the early 1950s as the best period
of Mao's rule. But in 1958 the "Great Leap Forward,"
the ideologically driven five-year plan to accelerate the
economy, marked the beginning of campaigns driven
by politics rather than pragmatism. Flooding and
drought in 1959 and 1960 led to famine; after the
Sino–Soviet split in 1960, the Soviet Union stopped
giving aid to China. In the mid-1960s, Deng Xiaoping
(who later became president) and Liu Shaoqi held
power. Free markets were encouraged, peasants were
allowed to own land, and the Soviet-influenced policies
that had failed so disastrously were, all too briefly,
abandoned.

The Cultural Revolution (1966–76)

Mao felt that China was slipping back into its capitalist

毛主席是我们心中的红太阳

ways, and in May 1966
he unleashed the "Great
Proletarian Cultural
Revolution," whose shock
troops were teenage Red
Guards. Its aim was "to
hold aloft the banner of
Mao Zedong's thought
. . . struggle against the
capitalist roaders . . .
transform education,

literature, and art . . . and facilitate the development of the socialist system." For ten years, until Mao's death from Parkinson's disease on September 9, 1976, China was engulfed in cruelty and orchestrated chaos. Schools and universities closed, teachers were humiliated and persecuted; anyone labeled an intellectual or a capitalist could be tortured, killed, or sent to labor in atrocious conditions; the only music allowed was one of so-called eight "Revolutionary Model Operas" that Mao's wife, Jiang Qing, considered suitably proletarian; bookshops sold "Quotations from Chairman Mao Zedong," widely known as Mao's Little Red Book, and very little else. Millions died, many committing suicide in despair. It is almost impossible to reconcile this decade of collective madness and brutality with today's vibrant, confident China, even more so because young Chinese people know very little about it—but it happened.

The Open Door Policy

Mao belatedly supported the efforts of Prime Minister

Zhou Enlai to restore order in 1970. A window of opportunity to stop the chaos opened in 1972 with President Nixon's visit to China. Eventually, one year after Mao's death and the arrest of his wife Jiang Qing and the other members of the infamous "Gang of Four," Deng Xiaoping, supreme survivor against the odds, returned to power.

Deng's greatest achievement was the "Open Door Policy" that put China back into the global community on which it had for so long turned its back. Deng was a pragmatist: his famous statement that "It does not matter what color the cat is, so long as it catches mice," was the antithesis of Mao's dogmatism. He introduced market incentives and encouraged foreign trade, and his successors have continued these policies.

Since 1979, China's economy has doubled roughly every seven-and-a-half years. After a century of trauma the Chinese are rebuilding a civil society, one which may even herald a golden age that they can enjoy now, not simply one about which they can only reminisce.

Modern China

Milestones at the end of the twentieth century were the pro-democracy protests in Tiananmen Square in 1989, which, though shocking, did not plunge China back into the turmoil many had feared; and the unexpectedly

peaceful handover of the British-leased territory of
Hong Kong back to Chinese rule in 1997. The twenty-
first century has produced more milestones: China's
entry into the World Trade Organization in 2001,
after fifteen years of negotiations, and its hosting
of the Olympics in 2008. China is setting up and
financing (with an initial capital of US $100 billion)
the Asian Infrastructure Investment Bank, to help
to finance construction
in other parts of Asia. It
will doubtless rival the
IMF and the World Bank,
seen by some in Asia as
dominated by Western
countries.

China is the most
populous country in the
world. For thirty years
after the founding of the
PRC in 1949, couples
were encouraged to
produce ever more infant
revolutionaries and the
population doubled. "The
more Chinese, the better,"
said Mao; so the traditional Chinese desire for big
families went unchecked until the adoption of the
One Child family policy in 1979. The government
tried by every possible means to enforce this
unpopular measure. By official estimates, it resulted
in "only" 25 million babies being born each year. But
the Chinese are living to a ripe old age, so there is a
lack of young workers to pay for increasing numbers

of senior citizens. In October 2015, the end of the One Child policy was announced and all families are now allowed to have two children.

New Towns for New Citizens
To ease the pressure on its swelling cities, the government is building much-needed brand-new ones. The number of cities with a population of more than 500,000 has increased from twelve to eighty-one. Beijing, Shanghai, and Chongqing are three of the most densely populated, with Shanghai clocking up a tremendous 7,000 people per square mile (2,700 per sq. km).

GOVERNMENT AND THE ECONOMY
Rich and Poor
In 1978 there were 250 million people living in abject poverty; this has now fallen to 7 percent (Gallup, 2012), poverty being defined as the number of people living on US $1.25 a day. However, income disparities have

increased. The growing income inequality is seen most clearly by the differences in living standards between the urban, coastal areas and the rural, inland regions. There have also been increases in the inequality of provision in health and education. Despite this, the increase in prosperity is undeniable. The World Bank estimates that by 2020 per-capita income in China will be approaching that of Portugal in the 1990s, even though that will still be less than half that of people in the United States.

THE POLITICAL LANDSCAPE

The Communist Party of China was founded on July 1, 1921 and has ruled China since October 1, 1949. Currently, it has more than 82.6 million members, which is 6.13 percent of the population. Membership of the Communist Party is no longer the prerequisite for getting a job, housing, or education that it once was. But nor is the Party democratically accountable, and China's economic progress has not been matched by political change. There are still many incidences of corruption, suppression of workers' protests, and human rights violations, many of which go unreported by the government controlled media.

Despite ongoing government attempts at stamping out corruption and malpractice, people often feel that their only recourse to justice is to take to the streets. These protests are known as "mass incidents," and official Chinese figures record many thousands of them every year. Visitors to Beijing's Forbidden

City may spot large groups who are obviously not tourists: they are petitioners, who travel to Beijing to try to regain land taken from them, or protest against non-payment of wages or other abuses. Half of the magnificent Forbidden City is a museum, but the other half is still used by the government. This is where petitioners from all over China have come since time immemorial—with mixed results.

China monitors the Internet and blocks sites it deems harmful to national (or Party) interests. The system is referred to as "The Great Firewall of China." Western sites such as YouTube, Facebook, and Google have been banned; search terms such as Falun Gong (a banned religious cult) are blocked. However, savvy Internet users keep one step ahead in this game of cat and mouse, and can gain anonymous access to banned Web sites. In addition, people increasingly use their cell phones to film events such as the huge explosion at the chemical plant in Tianjin in the summer of 2015; by uploading them directly onto the Internet they can bypass official censorship.

China can still seem very slow and bureaucratic; however, some things happen very quickly. For example, public planning enquiries for large infrastructure projects are niceties that do not bother the (unelected) government. In the UK, the argument over whether to approve the building of another runway at Heathrow or at Gatwick airport in London has rumbled on for decades. Meanwhile, China has built no fewer than a hundred new *airports* since 2011, many of them surrounded by brand new towns, roads, housing and, inevitably, gleaming new shopping malls. Some of these airport centered megacities have been inelegantly christened "aerotropolises," and they are enormous—one, for example, just outside the ancient city of Zhengzhou, 497 miles (800 km) south of Beijing, will house 2.6 million people by 2025.

Since the 1980s, the Chinese have had much more choice about where to live, where to go to school, how to dress, which job to take, whether to marry or stay single; and while gay marriage is not yet legal in China, being openly gay is no longer illegal. All these choices used to be made for them in the days when the Party ruled every single aspect of people's lives. As for businesses, they can have access to foreign currency and can make their own arrangements to meet foreign partners, produce a product, or travel abroad.

OTHER CHINESE COMMUNITIES

For years, English-language maps printed in China showed Hong Kong with the letters "oc. GB" after its name, meaning "occupied by Great Britain." Hong Kong, along with Portuguese "occupied" Macau, were handed back to the PRC in 1997 and 1999 respectively. Taiwan remains a sensitive topic, though there are many discreet business contacts between the PRC and the ROC (Republic of China), as Taiwan is also known.

Taiwan

Taiwan has its own democratically elected government, but only a handful of countries officially recognize it as a nation state and it does not have a seat at the United Nations. The island's politically dominant mainlanders were closely associated with Chiang Kai-shek's defeated Guomindang Party.

Hong Kong

Hong Kong has retained many features of traditional Chinese culture that were banned for years in the PRC, along with the vibrancy and the strong work ethic that have made it so successful economically. There is still a (relatively) free press, too, though it treads softly lest it tread on the mainland government's dreams. Many mainlanders go shopping in Hong Kong to buy foreign brands of baby milk and other food products, which they take back home and sell at a profit.

Macau

Macau was never as wealthy as Hong Kong; therein lay its unspoiled charm. The Portuguese practiced a relaxed form of colonialism, and thousands of Hong Kong Chinese would take the ferry over to Macau every weekend to indulge their passion for gambling. Gambling, along with many other previously forbidden pleasures, is allowed again in China, but Macau's casinos are as busy as ever. Some of its faded colonial charm has been swept away by brash new developments, but it is still a fascinating place to visit, by ferry across the South China Sea from Hong Kong, or by road from the mainland.

THE ENVIRONMENT
Pollution

Respiratory and heart disease related to air pollution are a major cause of death in China. Much energy production is still dependent on coal, and air pollution is so bad in major cities like Beijing that residents often do not see the sunlight for weeks on end. Waste from

factories and sewers is poured into China's rivers and lakes; much of the water is anaerobic, that is, devoid of oxygen and supporting no life at all, apart from algae. It is reckoned that the area of desert increases every year by about 950 square miles (2,460 sq. km).

Pollution is much discussed, both officially by government and unofficially by the millions who suffer its effects every day. In 2015, an online documentary about pollution in China called "Under the Dome" was uploaded onto the Chinese Internet and in 48 hours had 100 million views. Its producer was Chai Jing, a journalist, TV presenter, and new mother to a baby girl. Her daughter had been born with a tumor and Chai Jing was convinced that air pollution was to blame. She spent the year after her daughter's birth traveling around China, interviewing scientists and ordinary people. One memorable interview in the film is with a young woman who has never seen a real star, so thick is the smog in her native city.

The government is only too well aware of the problem. At the Climate Change conference in Paris in 2015, China joined 195 signatories committed to cutting emissions to reduce global warming. In September 2016, on the eve of the G20 leaders' summit in Hangzhou—the first G20 summit to be held in China—Presidents Xi Jinping and Barack Obama jointly announced the ratification of the Paris Agreement. China is moving away from coal and toward greener energy and has become not only the world's biggest manufacturer of solar panels, but also the world's biggest user of them. Solar panel farms in the hot, arid emptiness of the Gobi Desert, in northwest China, are the largest in the world. China's use of wind, hydro, and nuclear power sources is growing too, and it is increasingly involved with building new energy infrastructure in other countries.

Wildlife

China's huge population and economic boom have had a devastating impact on forests and wildlife. Confucian philosophy suggested nature was there to

be exploited by man and a conservation mindset has been slow to develop. It is depressing to walk through a food market in the south of the country, where tastes are less conservative than in the north, and see rare animals such as pangolins, racoons, and monkeys crammed into tiny cages, still alive, but destined for the pot. It is equally sad to look through the window of traditional medicine shops, where the dried remains of assorted threatened species are proudly displayed: traditional Chinese medicine uses tiger bones and musk deer antlers, powdered rhino horn, and the bile ducts of black bears. Ivory from the tusks of slaughtered elephants continues to be sold in China, too, despite attempts to stop it. In response the Chinese government points to its record of establishing over 300 nature reserves and its attempts to stop illegal poaching. Iconic species such as the panda are now protected; many others are not.

chapter two

VALUES & ATTITUDES

SCHOOLS OF THOUGHT

The history of China has been built on social order and the avoidance of chaos, or *luan*. The four major cultural factors that have influenced the development of its society in the past three millennia are the philosophies of Confucianism, Legalism, Daoism, and Maoism/Marxism.

Confucianism

The ethical system first laid down by Confucius in the sixth century BCE emphasized virtue, promotion on

merit by scholarship, devotion to the family, and justice. The essentially conservative tenets of the sage are now being invoked by the Communist Party in the interests of creating a more civilized, united nation, or, as the current catchphrase has it, a "harmonious society." For some, Confucianism is credited with helping China survive numerous difficulties, and its teachings are seen as compatible with the need for courtesy, justice, and honor.

But others consider Confucianism as a bulwark of feudalism and sexism.

Legalism
The Legalists had their moment of glory at the time of the Emperor Qin Shi Huang's reunification of the divided land in 221 BCE. To the Legalists, man was born sinful, and only the full force of law ruthlessly applied could quell his baser impulses.

Daoism
The joyful, irreverent, quietist philosophy of Daoism, enunciated by the sage Lao Zi (born about 570 BCE), rejected both the moral idealism of Confucianism and the laws of Legalism as products of social contrivance. For Daoists, justice flowed from living in a state of harmony with the natural world.

Marxism and Maoism
The writings of Karl Marx, which had such an influence on the nineteenth- and twentieth-century revolutionaries, were rooted in the rationalism of

the Enlightenment and the morality of the Judeo–Christian religious tradition. Dr. Sun Yat-sen and many early Chinese revolutionaries were equally influenced by Christian ideas of good and evil. Basic concepts of social equality and sharing wealth were fundamental to these early revolutionaries.

The Chinese Communist Party borrowed many ideas from its Soviet counterpart, and it  was not until 1949 that Mao Zedong's thought developed independently. Mao constantly urged the Chinese to identify with the peasants and with the poorer members of society, so the slogan "the poorer the better" became part of China's thinking in the 1950s, '60s, and '70s. People shunned personal adornment, such as jewelry, and if someone had a new jacket or pair of trousers, they would hide it under an old, torn one. The metaphor of the "iron rice bowl" was also part of Maoist philosophy. People were allocated a secure (but low-paid) job for life and an "iron rice bowl" that could never break; but the bowl contained only a small quantity of low-quality rice.

At first the Communists followed their own philosophy—but this self-denial did not last. By the 1960s, sheltered behind high walls, the new emperors were starting to partake of many of the pleasures of life that they did not allow anyone else to enjoy. The official Chinese verdict on Mao nowadays is that, as Deng Xiaoping said, he was

"70 per cent good, 30 per cent bad," and that the Cultural Revolution was "a mistake." Nevertheless, his portrait still hangs over the gateway to the Forbidden City, his embalmed body (according to popular rumor replaced several times by a waxwork) occupies a huge mausoleum in Tiananmen Square, and children still study his teachings in school. Mao's slogan "The poorer the better," has long been replaced by Deng Xiaoping's much more popular version, "To get rich is glorious"; yet it would still be considered discourteous for the visiting foreigner to criticize Mao, even though Chinese may do so in private. They should not do so in public, though. In April 2015, a video of a popular CCTV host called Bi Fujian was posted online. Foolishly, he had been filmed insulting Mao at a private dinner party. Mr. Bi apologized, but lost his job—though that is a mild punishment compared to what might have happened a few decades ago.

Yin and Yang

Chinese cosmology sees the universe as being divided into two opposing yet complementary aspects, the primal forces of *yin* and *yang*. Yin corresponds to earth, moon, female, cold, and dark, whereas Yang corresponds to heaven, sun, male, heat, and brightness. The dragon was the embodiment of Yang, and the sun is still known in everyday speech as the Great Yang (*tai yang*). As Yin and Yang alternate, so night is followed by day, and the seasons rotate. The pictorial representation of these polarities is a circle, containing a dark shape surrounding a bright nucleus, and its mirror image. It demonstrates that pure male and female do not exist: each contains its own opposite. This principle of balancing forces is embedded in Chinese philosophy.

Feng Shui

Feng is the Chinese word for wind; *shui* means water. It refers to the traditional Chinese belief that there are influences in the natural environment that affect people's fortunes. Every hill, field, and body of water is taken into account in matters such as the siting of graves, temples, homes, and, especially, offices. Since the skill needed for choosing an auspicious site is complex, families or organizations will call in a geomancer, often at considerable expense, before planning decisions are made. Whereas in the West proposals to build new houses or offices on open ground may be objected to on environmental or historical grounds, in southern China villagers still protest against a new building because it would damage the *feng shui* of the area.

PRAGMATISM

While old traditions are still important, the size of the Chinese population and the lack of a social security safety net means that most Chinese are pragmatists. They work and save hard to give their children a good education and help them get a decent job, find somewhere to live, improve their own level of culture and education, and—if there is any money left over—to travel and enjoy life. Young urban Chinese are very like their counterparts anywhere else in the world now—hedonistic, with more disposable income than their parents had and much more to spend it on, hardworking, but also fun loving, and not overly interested in China's bloodstained past.

Rural dwellers, too, have ambitions, and many have become rich. Millions have migrated to the towns where the factories that churn out all those desirable goods offer employment and an easier life; though when the factories close as demand slumps, or wages are not paid, there is little for the newly jobless migrants to do but return home, or wander on to another city. Though the country's newfound prosperity has been built on the back of an estimated 260 million rural migrants, they are in effect China's underclass. With no legal residency permits for the big cities, and no work back home in the impoverished towns and villages where they do have the right to live, they are often trapped. But they are fighting back; there were an estimated 1,300 strikes and protests across China in 2014, up from 185 in 2011. The government passed labor laws in 1995, stipulating the right to a decent wage, rest periods, no excessive overtime, and the right to group negotiation, but at the same time strikes are only allowed through a government-approved trade union and are frequently broken up by the police. The official Xinhua news agency frequently reports on the problems of migrant workers, especially on their lack of benefits, such as pensions and housing subsidies. Ironically, there is a risk that if Chinese workers succeed in gaining better salaries, rights, and benefits, the factories that have employed them at low wages will simply move elsewhere, to Vietnam, Indonesia, and Myanmar, just as once companies moved to China away from Europe and the USA.

LOSING FACE

The Confucian emphasis on social conformity means that most Chinese are highly sensitive about losing face, in other words, being made to look foolish in front of other people, especially in front of a foreigner. If they cannot answer a difficult question, they may laugh to cover their embarrassment. It could mean that the visitor has said something that has not been understood, or that the Chinese person is unsure of his ground on some point. Equally, a foreigner loses face by becoming angry or upset. The phrase "It is not convenient" is often polite code for saying that something is impossible, or difficult, but that the Chinese person would rather not explain all the niceties of the situation at that moment. It is possible to push gently at this seemingly closed door, but do *not* try to kick it down. It is not rude to come back to a problem at a later stage, when there has been time for the Chinese person to discuss the issue privately with other people.

THE MYTH OF CHINESE "INSCRUTABILITY"

Western writers often used to say that Chinese people were not given to being direct in conversation, and favored an oblique approach to almost all subjects; in fact you will probably find that the Chinese people you meet, while treating you very courteously, are often more direct than Westerners. Once they know and trust you they are as ready to show emotion as anyone else. You can expect to be asked direct and detailed questions about your age, family, marital status, health, housing, car, and salary—and you, in turn, can ask them about the same sorts of things. But take your cue from them; some people are more curious than others and will not mind if you reciprocate in kind.

PATIENCE IS A VIRTUE: KEEP CALM
In the PRC there can be a lot of red tape involved in what might seem the simplest of procedures—buying tickets, or changing money at a bank, for example—and it is essential to learn to accept such inconveniences gracefully. Impatience is seen as a serious character flaw, and anyway is counterproductive. A local fixer or just a good Chinese friend will be invaluable in helping you through these transactions.

ATTITUDES TOWARD THE FAMILY
The family unit is key to every individual's place in Chinese society. Children are idolized when they are small and it is usual for older people to live with their children and grandchildren as long as their health allows.

Babies and Children
The Chinese adore their own babies and children, and Westerners traveling with their children will find them the center of attention. It can be a bit overwhelming for very young Western children to have their cheeks pinched and their arms stroked almost beyond

endurance. They may have to pose for endless selfies with their hordes of fans (children with curly blond or red hair especially can attract huge crowds in minutes).This deep-seated Chinese love of children comes partly from the belief in the need for family continuity, but also from sheer joy in their freshness and newly minted enthusiasm in a country where life is still hard for many.

RESPECT FOR OLD AGE AND ANCESTORS
Another effect of the Confucian stress on filial piety is the respect shown to older people and to more distant ancestors. Most Westerners have heard vaguely of the slightly sinister sounding "ancestor worship," but it simply means showing respect for one's ancestors; the springtime festival of Qing Ming, when families bring offerings to the tombs of their ancestors, has regained its traditional importance after being

supressed in Mao's time. One drawback of this tradition of venerating old age is that, until recently, anyone who held a position of power was more or less guaranteed to keep the job till he (it usually was a "he") died in office or retired reluctantly at about eighty-five. This did not do much for the country's economy, or the chances of promotion of younger people with fresh new ideas. But as the free-market economy takes over, older people are happy enough to retire earlier and enjoy life, with the prospect of a small pension and of spending time with their grandchildren replacing the old one of continued drudgery till the day they died.

RESPECT FOR EDUCATION

The Chinese have always valued learning and respected scholars. One of the worst effects of Mao's 1966–76 Cultural Revolution was that a whole generation lost

out on schooling. Nowadays, people are even more passionate about education as they move toward a modern, knowledge-based economy. Chinese school children and university students have enormous amounts of homework, and have to take very tough and competitive exams. Teachers and professors are once again highly respected (though not highly paid). Parents are increasingly expected to help out and many state schools now charge fees. Online teaching and distance education on the TV and radio are also provided—ideal for such a huge country. In the poorer regions, access to primary education has improved, though secondary education is not so easily available.

One of the consequences of greater wealth and personal freedom in China (and arguably one of the better effects of the One Child policy) is that many Chinese parents have been able to save enough money to send their only sons and daughters overseas to study. The number of Chinese students overseas in 2014 was almost 460,000 according to the Chinese Ministry of Education. The USA, Canada, Australia, New Zealand, and the UK are all top destinations for these young scholars, about one third of whom are heading to secondary schools, the rest to university.

The number of foreign students coming to China is also rising every year, up to nearly 378,000 in 2014, mainly from South Korea, the USA, Thailand, Russia, and Japan. Most come to learn Chinese, though some study medicine, engineering, finance, and economics.

GUANXI, OR NETWORKING, CHINESE STYLE

Networking, or *guanxi*, was for centuries the main way of getting anything done—finding a marriage partner, a school or job for your child, a market for your product, a place to live, or a trip overseas. Favors were given and returned in an unspoken web of complex relationships. On the whole, it is family ties that form the basis of Chinese *guanxi* because of the moral obligation of relatives to help each other, but non-relatives and foreigners can be incorporated into the network. The overseas Chinese have long appreciated the value of such links in business, in minimizing the uncertainties of economic relationships. But the foreign visitor to China should be aware that accepting favors carries an expectation that these will be reciprocated one day. Worse still, trying to build *guanxi* by offering expensive gifts or trips abroad can end up being considered as a form of bribery by the Chinese government, which has been running a fierce anti-corruption campaign.

ATTITUDES TOWARD RELIGION

China is officially secular, but tolerant of organized religions so long as they do not threaten the rule of the Communist Party. Most Chinese combine a love of traditions (often called folk religion) with a practical, materialistic atheism. But faced with a moral vacuum as Marxism fades into the background, organized religions are growing in popularity; see Chapter 3 for more details.

ATTITUDES TOWARD THE STATE

From infancy onward Chinese education encourages people to be patriotic, not too questioning of the Communist Party's hold on power, and to strive to create a "harmonious society," based on the avoidance of chaos and the awareness of one's rightful place in the cosmos. The current government has roped in Confucius to help keep order, though his ideas were rejected as feudal under Mao; and of course the Party controls the media at all levels. But even more important for continued social harmony is the government's ability to provide food, jobs, housing, health care, and shops full of everything people could want, plus increased personal freedom. So long as all these boxes are ticked, which they have been during the period of rapid economic growth, people on the whole are happy to go along with the status quo. Dissident voices are firmly discouraged though, and people tend not to criticize the government. The dread

of "chaos" (social unrest) is still strong, and the shared vision of a "harmonious society" is a powerful one.

CULTURAL SUPERIORITY

In the past, the Chinese were told they lived in a perfect society and they mostly believed it, having nothing with which to compare it. The Chinese are proud of their country, but are fairly realistic about its problems, now that they can travel and surf the Internet. Ironically, the main evening news bulletin (pre-recorded, as live broadcasts are considered too risky) on China Central TV every evening still focuses on how well China is doing, while broadcasting footage showing that abroad (in other words, on the fringes of empire) people are fighting and killing each other, while suffering from floods, fire, pestilence, and incompetent governments. The format and the message feel about forty years out of date, which is probably why few people take it seriously as a news source any more.

ATTITUDES TOWARD WOMEN

One of the Communists' slow but fairly successful campaigns has been to try and give women in Chinese society equal rank with men. There is still a traditional preference for sons over daughters among some people; this preference led to selective female infanticide, an ancient "feudal" practice, constantly condemned by the government, but which has proved surprisingly hard to stamp out. In the days before ultrasound scans, an unwanted baby girl was

killed after being born—nowadays it can be done more scientifically beforehand, but either way the practice has led to an imbalance of boys over girls, and predictions of millions of lonely bachelors.

Progress

In 1949, when the Communists took power, the barbaric tradition of binding women's feet to keep them from growing "big and ugly" was still in force, despite earlier efforts to ban it in 1912. As recently as the 1980s, it was common to see elderly ladies with tiny feet hobbling around; thirty years on, that generation has gone. However many Chinese women still consider bare feet to be ugly and wear thin socks to hide them, even in the hot summers, where Westerners would probably go barefooted.

Another genuine "great leap forward" for women in the PRC has been the availability of free contraception and state-funded childcare. Mao's statement that "women hold up half the sky" is slowly coming true, as a whole generation of young, clever, educated women take their place in the world of commerce, science, medicine, and the media. Progress for women is slower in the rarefied atmosphere of Chinese politics. But foreign women traveling in China or working there will be accepted on equal terms.

ATTITUDES TOWARD SEX

The widespread availability of contraception and sexual health clinics, plus a general acceptance of women's equality and of homosexuality, means that attitudes toward sex are fairly free and easy, though most young Chinese men and women

still prefer to date just one person whom they see as a partner for life. Nightclubs and gay bars in big cities (but not in the countryside) mean the visiting foreigner need never be lonely if he or she fancies some company. Take your own contraceptives, though; the ones you buy in China may not always be reliable.

ATTITUDES TOWARD OVERSEAS CHINESE

Pressure of population, conflicts, and economic woes meant that for centuries there was a steady flow of people leaving China. The earliest emigrants were traders and craftsmen who moved to Southeast Asia, where they continue to play a dominant role in business. In the nineteenth century, laborers or "coolies"(from the Chinese words *ku li*, or "bitter strength") were recruited in large numbers from south China for work in British, French, and Dutch colonies, and in the Americas. By the 1930s, there were nearly ten million overseas Chinese; many have sent money back to their families, invested in factories, and endowed universities in China. Nonetheless, the attitude of the mainland Chinese to their overseas cousins is often a toxic mixture of resentment and grudging admiration, and it can be hard for them to be accepted.

ATTITUDES TOWARD FOREIGNERS

Unlike Western societies with their growing cultural diversity, Chinese society is very homogenous; though unequal economically, almost everyone shares a similar outlook and racial background. But this does not mean individual Chinese are racist. You may occasionally hear yourself referred to by the derogatory term *yang gweize*, or "foreign devil" (*gweilo* in Cantonese), but with the influx of people from around the world this old-fashioned attitude is disappearing. Nowadays, the educated urban middle classes of all ages tend to be pleased to meet anyone from other countries, of whatever race; in remoter regions, an initial wariness is quickly replaced by delighted excitement. This can have its downside for the lone foreigner, who, especially if he or she is traveling with small children, can rapidly start to feel like an exhibit at a freak show—or a minor celebrity. The corollary to all this attention is that when the lone foreigner (and their much admired small children) returns home, they have to get used to being completely ignored.

From the 1970s onward many students from Africa came to Chinese universities. Some told of the reaction to their skin color when they walked along the street. Chinese migrant workers from rural areas would come up to them and rub away at their arms, genuinely puzzled, then say "Why don't you go home and wash this coal dust off you?" Today, with TV and the Internet having filled in the gaps in people's knowledge of the world, people of color are usually greeted like any other foreigners, warmly and with interest, and are no longer asked why they have failed to wash—though they may be quizzed about American basketball teams.

chapter three

CUSTOMS & TRADITIONS

MANY RELIGIONS AND NONE

For a secular country, China has a large number of religions, all happily coexisting. All the great world religions are found here; Confucianism, Taoism, and Buddhism have traditionally shaped Chinese culture and elements of each have been incorporated into what is loosely called "folk religion." As well as these traditional belief systems, which for the Western visitor have come to epitomize China, Islam and Christianity are making a comeback—a situation that, while tolerated by the ruling Communist Party, is also

being cautiously watched. The government occasionally cracks down on cults like the Falun Gong sect, which is perceived as a threat, though to Western eyes they are just eccentric, harmless people looking for meaning in their lives. The government has also pulled down crosses on Christian churches when it felt they were getting too numerous; and arrested people who run "house churches," rather than worshiping in officially approved buildings.

In other words, religion is tolerated when it is possible to monitor it and check it is not secretly conspiring to overthrow the ruling party, as has happened throughout Chinese history.

Buddhism

Buddhism is the main religion of Tibet, where "overzealous" (in the government's view) nuns and monks have been imprisoned and much worse. Outside Tibet, Buddhism is taken less seriously. Brightly painted Buddhist temples are crowded with people busily "kowtowing" (touching heads to the ground) and lighting incense, but there is also a lot of irreverent laughter and many selfies being taken at the same time.

Islam

Islam is the chief religion in China's northwestern province of Xinjiang; it is thought that only about 1–2 percent of the population is Muslim. However, this is China, so even that low percentage translates to around 20 to 30 million followers of Islam. Further away from the capital, in the far northwest of China, women wear the hijab and mosques are busy, but the extreme form of Islam found in Saudi Arabia and other countries is apparently absent from China.

Christianity

Christianity in China is booming; according to *The Economist*'s China correspondent, in 2014 there were about 57,000 officially approved churches around the country. Chinese churches are very different from the Western image of a church as an ancient stone building with a dwindling elderly congregation, worshiping in ways unchanged for centuries. Churches in China are large, modern buildings where as many as 5,000 people, mostly young, come to take part in enthusiastic evangelical-style worship, often with an orchestra and choir. There are thought to be between 23 to 40 million Christians in China and the number is growing. The reason seems to be that Christianity has stepped in to replace Marxism as a readymade moral system, seen by some as a force capable of upholding civil society.

Judaism

Jews first came to China in the seventh century during the reign of the Tang dynasty. The most famous Jewish community settled in Kaifeng, in Henan province, and for a while were thought to be one of the lost tribes of Israel. Jewish refugees and merchants came to Hong Kong, Shanghai, and Harbin throughout the first half of the early twentieth century. Many of the earliest settlers have been absorbed into the mainstream Chinese population and do not even know of their Jewish ancestry.

NATIONAL HOLIDAYS (SOLAR CALENDAR)	
New Year's Day	January 1–3
Spring Festival (Lunar New Year)	February 7–13 (seven days)
International Women's Day	March 8
Labor Day	April 30–May 2
Chinese Youth Day	May 4
Children's Day	June 1
Army Day	August 1
Teachers' Day	September 10
National Day	October 1 (three days)
TRADITIONAL FESTIVALS (LUNAR CALENDAR)	
Chun Jie, Chinese New Year/ Spring Festival	Coincides with the new moon in late January/early February
Yuan Xiao Jie, Lantern Festival	First full moon after Spring Festival
Qing Ming Jie, Pure Brightness Day	Third day of the third month in Spring
Duan Wu Jie, Dragon Boat Festival	Fifth day of fifth lunar month
Zhong Qiu Jie, Mid-Fall Festival	Fifteenth day of the eighth lunar month

Public holiday dates are announced before the start of the year by the General Office of the State Council. These are for 2016.

HIGH DAYS AND HOLIDAYS

The Chinese use a mixture of the same Gregorian calendar as in the West, combined with their own lunisolar calendar, based on precise calculations of the sun's position and the moon's phases. The PRC and the

Chinese diaspora use the lunisolar calendar to decide on the dates of festivals and to choose auspicious days for weddings, funerals, moving house, or starting a new business. Unlike in the Gregorian calendar, the same month can be of different lengths in different years. Months begin on the "day of the dark moon" and end the day before the next "dark moon," and the year runs from one winter solstice to the next.

The, less exotic, official PRC holidays are: Labor Day on May 1, Chinese Youth Day on May 4, Army Day on August 1, National Day on October 1, and New Year's Day on January 1.

National Day's traditional parades along the main streets of Beijing still take place, but are less militaristic than they were; more important is that people get time off and are encouraged to go out and spend money. Judging by the crowds in the shops, they are only too happy to oblige. If you go to China on National Day or around the Chinese New Year, you will have trouble finding anyone in their offices.

Christmas Day is an ordinary working day in China, though it is a holiday in Hong Kong and Macau. Christmas, Chinese style, has been adopted enthusiastically in the big cities, with Santa Claus and shopping as its main rationale; in the countryside and the western areas, where Islam and Buddhism are stronger influences, Christmas is virtually unheard of.

Just as in the West, St Valentine's Day, Easter, Halloween, and Christmas are seen by business as opportunities to make money, so in China traditional holidays such as the Spring Festival combine shopping, big family reunions, and some picturesque old traditions.

Chinese New Year

Spring Festival, or Chinese New Year, is the most important holiday and is also marked in other Asian countries. It falls around the beginning of February, traditionally a quiet time in the farming year. This is the time for family reunions; trains are packed with migrant workers and students heading home. People dress in new clothes, and set off strings of noisy firecrackers at all hours of the day and night, supposedly to scare away evil spirits.

Families gather to make and eat stuffed dumplings called *jiaozi*, shaped like gold ingots to bring good luck. Younger members of the family pay their respects to the older members (and, in more traditional homes, to the ancestors as well) and the children are given small red envelopes of money. Houses are decorated with New Year pictures and

rhyming couplets written on red paper. (Red is a lucky color in China.) This may also be the occasion to watch a Lion Dance, for all-night gambling sessions, and for paying off debts.

THE CHINESE CALENDAR

Each year in the lunar calendar is named after a particular animal from the Chinese horoscope, and there are twelve altogether. A Chinese person will always be able to tell you that he or she was born in the year of the Tiger, Horse, or whatever. The order in which the twelve-year cycle repeats itself is: Rat, Ox, Tiger, Hare, Dragon, Snake, Horse, Sheep (or Goat), Monkey, Cock, Dog, and Pig. So the years of the Dragon have been 1952, 1964, 1976, 1988, 2000, 2012, and the next one will be in 2024. Just as the different star signs in the Western horoscope have certain characteristics associated with them, so do the Chinese animals.

Qing Ming Festival

On the festival of Qing Ming, which takes place on the third day of the third month in the spring, families visit the tombs of their ancestors, clean them, and make symbolic offerings of joss paper, cooked meats, fish, fruit, and wine. They then picnic on the food themselves, sitting near the tombs. Many families used to have their own ancestral halls where wooden tablets inscribed with the names of their male ancestors were kept, but thousands were destroyed by Mao's Red Guards in the 1960s. From these tablets, families could be traced back several hundred years or even more. In the town of Qufu, where Confucius was born, almost the whole town seems to have the same surname as his—Kong—and can therefore trace their families back to about 500 BCE.

Dragon Boat Festival

The Dragon Boat Festival (*Duan Yang Jie*, or *Duan Wu Jie*) falls on the fifth day of the fifth lunar month. It is associated with Qu Yuan, a loyal minister of Chu

(an ancient state in the south of China) in the third
century BCE, who committed suicide by jumping into
a local river when the King of Chu refused to listen
to his good advice. There are races between long,
thin "dragon boats" to the rhythm of drums, said to
represent attempts to rescue Qu Yuan from the river.
Packets of glutinous rice (*zongzi*) wrapped in leaves are
eaten; these are said to have been decoys for the fish
(or, in some versions, the dragon) so that they would
eat the rice rather than devour the hapless Qu Yuan.

The Moon Festival
This occurs on the fifteenth day of the eighth lunar
month (around mid-September), when the moon is
supposed to be brighter than at any other time of the
year. It is equivalent to the Western Harvest Festival,
and celebrates the legend of the moon goddess,
Chang-O. This, too, is a festival when the family gets
together, sitting around a circular table to symbolize
continuity, possibly to sing folk songs (now replaced

by karaoke), or to display fancy lanterns, but mostly to admire the full moon and eat "moon-cakes." These are round cakes stuffed with lotus-seed paste, or fruit, ham, or egg: the fillings vary. Another legend intertwined with the Moon Festival tells how Chinese rebels seeking to overthrow the Mongols during the Yuan dynasty sent coded messages hidden inside moon cakes.

"LONELY HEARTS" SHOPPING SPREE

Singles Day is a brand new festival, invented in 2009 by China's Alibaba Web site purely as a marketing ploy, which (according to BBC News) has rapidly become "the world's biggest online retail event." The chosen date is November 11, or 11/11, the four number ones symbolizing four "bare sticks," in other words, lonely singletons. It falls conveniently in the middle of a quiet trading period, and is such a hit that Alibaba have copyrighted the term "Double 11." By 2013, sales on Singles' Day outstripped those in the US on their nearest equivalent, Black Friday.

LIFE'S MILESTONES
Symbols of Long Life and Happiness

Foods, symbols, and rituals that promise long life are greatly valued. Noodles are often eaten on the day of someone's birthday, their long strands

symbolizing long life. A perfect, rounded peach is another symbol of long life, often seen in folk art, as are the tortoise, deer, and the crane. The figure of a long-legged crane with its wings outspread is used during funeral processions; the bird is thought to carry the dead person up to heaven. Nowadays these traditions are very much in the background, but are still valued when people celebrate or grieve.

Births

The birth of a child, particularly a son, is regarded as a lucky event; continuity of the family is assured and a feast is held a month after the child's birth, in which hard-boiled eggs with the shells dyed red are eaten. By the traditional calendar, age is reckoned from the moment of conception, not birth, so a child is already considered to be one year old on the day it is born. Birthdays as such are not much celebrated in China. There is a birthday for "everyone," which falls on the seventh day of the Chinese New Year.

Weddings

Weddings in China have always been colorful and expensive occasions; the traditional color for weddings is red, though brides often nowadays hire white Western-style dresses to pose for the inevitable photos. Today at least most modern brides and grooms get to choose their own partners. In the past, the family chose for them, and the bride and groom would only see each other on the day of the wedding. Traditionally, the one aim of a girl's life was to get married; men, too, had a duty to perpetuate the family line. Before a marriage, a matchmaker would be employed to sort out the details of what was basically a financial transaction. When all had been agreed, the bride (often no more

than fourteen years old) would be conveyed from her parents' home though the streets in a sedan chair to the house of her new husband. No one would see her—the sedan chair was completely sealed, and there are stories of brides being found dead from suffocation on arrival (which did not stop the "marriage" from taking place). Another tradition, which the Communists put an end to, was that of the man taking concubines, either to give him more children, or simply because he grew bored with his first wife. In Tibet this custom worked in the opposite direction; polyandry, where one woman had several husbands, usually brothers, was common.

Funerals
The Chinese do not need to come to terms with their own mortality; they accept it as one of the most important events in the life cycle. White is worn at funerals and if the deceased has made it to seventy years old—the same age that the Bible gives as man's natural life span—there is not thought to be any reason for serious grief, though there will be a lot of ritual lamentation during the funeral procession.

In an echo of the old custom of burying clothing and jewels with the body, entire shops are devoted to selling paper money, paper furniture, cars, houses, and paper clothes that are burned and placed with the body on burial. Even the non-religious will often pay a Buddhist or Daoist priest to say prayers and perform ceremonies for the soul of the dead person.

Traditionally the Chinese believed that the body had to go into the next world intact or its ghost would never be at peace; so cremation is unpopular (organ donation even more so). But China needs to find space to bury 9 million people a year and in the overcrowded cities there simply is not enough space for graveyards: in Shanghai for example, a plot of land for a grave can cost as much as 24,000 RMB (about US $3,573/£2,500). Cremating the body, then burying the ashes is one compromise. In 2013 a report in the *China Daily* described how the ever practical Chinese government is offering a new pathway to the afterlife: state subsidized burial of bodies at sea, using a fleet of special sea burial ships. The chosen day for these mass burials at sea is the Qing Ming holiday, the traditional day for tomb sweeping and ancestor visiting, and they are becoming quite popular. According to the report depositing one's loved one's remains at sea also means they cannot be stolen or disturbed.

chapter four

MAKING FRIENDS

Friendships with Chinese people are, perhaps contrary to a visitor's expectations, relatively easy to form and can last a lifetime. The number of foreigners resident in China is reckoned at about 845,000 (2013 figures)—a tiny percentage of the huge population. This is not counting tourists, of whom there were about 26 million in 2015 according to Chinese government figures. So as a foreigner you have scarcity value, and if you make a small effort to meet and befriend local people they will be only too pleased. Whether it is through work, while backpacking, through going out to bars, concerts, or clubs, or through dating and friendship Web sites, you may rapidly find that you are in such demand that you may have to rein back your overtures. People want to practice their English, get ideas from you about traveling or working overseas, and generally just experience the thrill of talking to someone from another, non-Chinese, world.

But beware: centuries of living under a capricious central state means people rely on each other more than any external power, so the bonds of friendship are taken seriously and you must not let your new friends down; it is best to play things a little cool at first and not make promises you cannot keep.

Most visitors to China tend to mix socially with the urban, middle-class Chinese, who have more in common with the average Westerner than with the rural inhabitants of their own country. Although the Western visitor will meet other people on his or her travels, conversation will be rather limited; first, because of the huge gulf in knowledge of the wider world, and second, because of the language barrier. Even if you learn enough Chinese to carry on a simple conversation, regional dialects outside the big cities can be pretty impenetrable.

MEETING AND GREETING

On meeting someone, of either sex and any age apart from very young children, the usual practice is to shake hands, often for a much longer time than would be usual in the West. If you are being introduced to a group of people, make sure to shake hands with each one of them.

In China it is rude not to stand up and shake hands when a new person enters the room. Wait until they have asked you to sit down before you collapse back into your armchair—formal meetings and informal gatherings in China often take place in rooms where armchairs are lined up, with military precision, around the walls of the room. When in doubt in China, err on the side of formality.

INVITATIONS HOME

In today's more relaxed political climate, it is increasingly common for the Chinese to invite their foreign friends home for dinner and the visit can be carried out quite openly. No Party vigilante will be hovering at the entrance to the apartment building inquiring whom you are visiting—though curious neighbors may well take on this role for themselves. Chinese people inviting Westerners to their home may invite relatives, neighbors, and friends to drop in and chat to the exotic visitor.

Entertainment usually takes place at the weekend as both husband and wife normally work and, with the need to do shopping on the way home, the day away from home can be a long one. In addition, schoolchildren have a lot of homework, and the arrival of a foreign visitor during the working week would not be conducive to study.

Chinese homes rarely have carpets underfoot, and floors are swept rather than vacuumed. Many

families remove their shoes inside their homes—take your cue from your hosts. The Chinese are extremely hospitable, and drinks will be served the moment the guest walks through the door, usually accompanied by snacks such as rice crackers and roasted watermelon or sunflower seeds. A meal will follow, which your hosts will have taken much time and trouble to prepare: though Chinese food is cooked very fast (thereby retaining its flavor and vitamins), the stages prior to it hitting the sizzling *wok* (the deep frying pan used to cook Chinese food) are quite laborious.

GIFT GIVING

If you are invited to someone's home it is polite to bring a small gift. When Chinese visitors come to the West they bring a number of small, typically Chinese presents for their hosts, and this is a good custom to imitate. Bring small decorative items typical of your country if you can; whiskey and foreign cigarettes, or an English-language book, would also be welcome. One of the results of China's westernization is that people have developed a sweet tooth, and so chocolates are welcome, as are flowers or plants (but not white ones; see overleaf). If the present is wrapped, many Chinese people will not unwrap it while their visitor is there, but will stow it away hurriedly out of sight. This does not mean they are displeased with it; it is simply "not done" to open the gift in front of the donor.

Some Dos and Don'ts
Do not give your Chinese friends a clock or a watch, as the words sound similar to "take someone to their death." Other gifts to avoid are sharp objects, symbolizing the end of a friendship; handkerchiefs, usually reserved for the end of a funeral; pears, because the word for them, *li*, sounds like the word for parting; yellow chrysanthemums and any white flowers, as they too are seen at funerals; umbrellas, *san* in Chinese as the word sounds like another *san*, meaning to break up; and mirrors, which are believed to attract ghosts. If you wrap your present in red paper it will symbolize happiness and good luck.

TIMEKEEPING
Whether joining a new friend for a meal, going to an old friend's house, or taking part in a business meeting, punctuality is vital. The Chinese consider it rude to be late. Chinese people rise early and go to bed early, so lunch will probably be at noon and evening meals are likely to begin around 6:00 p.m. Meals, meetings, and visits end promptly. Once the meal is over the guests may chat for a few minutes but should then get up and go. It is polite for your hosts to come all the way to the exit or to see you into your taxi to say good-bye, and if you are the host you should do the same.

MEN AND WOMEN
If you are dealing with someone of the opposite sex, there is unlikely to be any physical contact after the initial (very long and firm) handshake, but members

of the same sex do tend to touch each other more than in the West, and women frequently emphasize a point by stroking or patting each other. It is rare for people to kiss non-family members in China, though hugging friends (but not colleagues) is much more popular than it was.

Dating
Usually when a Chinese girl and boy start dating, it is assumed that they will get married. Visiting Westerners who date Chinese people should be aware of this—what they may see as a casual affair is likely to be taken much more seriously by their Chinese partner, who may expect that what for them is a "serious" love affair will lead to marriage. The attraction of life in the West is strong, and it is easy for foreigners unwittingly to abuse their power. Other than that, there are no special rules to follow, except to remember that social drinking plays a much less important role in Chinese society (especially for

women), and that young Chinese women expect to be treated with a more old-fashioned sense of chivalry than their Western counterparts. When Western women date Chinese men they usually say that they find the man kind and considerate. He will have been educated to think of women as equals; or even as superiors, since years of selective female infanticide have led to a shortage of marriageable women, on top of which Chinese women are now outperforming men at school and university.

Gay China

In recent years attitudes toward homosexuality have become much more relaxed; in the cities it is almost fashionable for men to be gay. This trend is sometimes explained as a reaction to the shortage of marriageable young women, but it seems more likely that it is because there is no longer any stigma attached to being openly gay, for men or women. Compared to many other societies China is now fairly relaxed about sexual freedoms, straight or gay.

SENSITIVE TOPICS

In private, and once people know and trust you, they will talk freely. However, it is best to avoid mentioning the "three Ts": Tibet, Taiwan, and Tienanmen Square. Tibet is considered to be a part of China, and any foreigner referring to it as a (would-be) independent country is met by bewilderment. Mention of the second "T," Taiwan, is equally futile; and few people in China, apart from those who were there between June 4 and 6, 1989, know what actually happened in

Beijing's Tienanmen Square, when popular protests were brutally suppressed by the army. In Hong Kong, however, hundreds of thousands commemorate the anniversary publicly every year.

CHINESE NAMES

In China the surname precedes the personal name, since the family group or clan is more important than the individual. Zhang Hua is thus Mr. Zhang, not Mr. Hua. However, sometimes the Chinese adopt the Western practice of putting the personal name before their surname. So it is a good idea, especially with a Chinese name of only two syllables, such as Jing Wang, to check whether the bearer of that name is a Mr./Ms. Jing, or a Mr./Ms. Wang. Only thirty surnames have two syllables; the rest are of one syllable only, and some of the commonest are Zhang, Wang, Wu, Zhao, and Li.

In addressing the Chinese people you meet it is best to use Mr., Mrs., Miss, plus their surnames: Chinese people are more formal than many Westerners. The all-purpose title used by the Communists, *Tong Zhi*, or "Comrade," has dropped out of use and older honorifics have come back into fashion, such as the Chinese equivalents of Sir/Madam/Miss.

The Chinese often refer to one another by job titles, such as Mayor Wang, Manager Li, Teacher Zhang, Engineer Zhou, and so on. This is how they normally refer to one another in Chinese, and is a useful habit to adopt. If you are working in China, they may well refer politely to you in the same way.

"Everyman"
An affectionate nickname for the Chinese peasant is *Lao Bai Xing*, or "Old Hundred Names." There are in fact four-hundred-and-thirty-eight Chinese surnames, but that is still a small number considering the size of the Chinese population.

The sound and the meanings of names are very important in China. If you can find a kind person to think up a good Chinese name for you, which fits your Western name phonetically and carries a positive meaning, then your name card will have more impact. People who have studied English often choose English names for themselves, which can be pleasingly old fashioned, such as William or Emily; equally, they often choose rather strange names from popular foreign films such as *Star Wars*.

Chinese children do not use their father's or mother's personal name, and in more old-fashioned families the wife and husband do not do so either. If a foreign visitor of the opposite sex uses the wife's or husband's personal name it can be embarrassing. So if you have a friend called Professor Zhang Dai Lin, call him or her (many names can belong to either a man or a woman in China) Professor Zhang, not Dai Lin, at least not until you know him or her very well indeed.

Another acceptable way of addressing people is to use their surname and the word *xiao* or *lao* in front of it. *Xiao* means "little" or "young"; *lao* means "old." The cut-off point is around thirty-five; so if

Mrs Hu and Mr Li
A custom that seems specially designed to bamboozle the foreigner is that most Chinese women do not change their surnames when they marry. It is possible to know Mrs. Hu and Mr. Li for a long time without realizing that they are actually married to each other!

you are a foreigner who starts visiting China when you are still *Xiao* Smith, one day you will have to get used to being called *Lao* Smith. Just remember that the Chinese are showing respect for your advancing age, even though you had rather hoped no one would notice it. Using *xiao* and *lao* is acceptable among friends and colleagues, and foreigners find it a welcome way to handle the intricacies of Chinese names. As for your own name, in business dealings it may be best to call yourself Mr. Smith, Miss Jones, or Mrs. Evans; keep the use of your first name for friends and colleagues when you know them better.

Last, not Least
When someone is really old the word *lao* is still used—but its position changes and the word *lao* goes after the family name, not before it. Toward the end of his long life, China's late president Deng Xiaoping (1904–97) was known respectfully as "Deng Lao."

chapter five

PRIVATE & FAMILY LIFE

THE FAMILY UNIT

In the West, the traditional family (two married parents, two children) is constantly said to be "in crisis." In China it is regarded as the basis of society and of the individual's guarantee of happiness and security. Rigid rules about premarital sex are relaxing, but unmarried mothers are rare, divorce rates are low (though rising fast), and looking after elderly family members at home rather than exiling them to an old people's "home" is almost universal.

In southern China especially, the family is often part of a much larger clan, whose duty is to help each other. Children are expected to show respect to their parents; this is the fundamental concept of filial piety as defined by Confucius: "Filial piety is the basis of all virtue. It begins with one's parents, is kept by serving one's sovereign, and ends up by establishing oneself [in life]." Some commentators feel that the One Child policy has had a negative effect on filial piety, creating a generation of children who are worshiped by their adoring parents, and who, because they have no siblings, have not had to learn the tedious early lessons of sharing. The Chinese have dubbed these children "little emperors," and they can be seen everywhere

practicing "pester power," that is, getting their parents to buy them things. However, much of this is just down to the Chinese love of small children; by the time the little emperors start school, being an only child puts them under considerable pressure to fulfil singlehandedly all their family's hopes.

In the remoter rural areas, family life is less focused on the needs of one small person, more on the need of the whole household to pull together to create wealth (or just to survive). The Chinese language has a whole range of kinship terms that show the position of different family members and their age—small brother is *didi*, big brother *gege*, and so on. Although the extended family is shrinking in the towns, these lovely old words should survive because many of them are also used for other people outside the immediate family, rather as in the West children used to call adult family friends "auntie " and "uncle."

Sadly, there has in recent years been a rise in the kidnapping of babies and very young children in China. Babies are sold to childless couples; older children to work in factories, as prostitutes, or as child beggars. China now has a national anti-kidnapping taskforce, and, according to journalist Charles Cluster: "Every year, this taskforce carries out high-profile raids and liberates hundreds, sometimes thousands, of kidnapped children." One result of this depressing trend is increased security in people's homes, and the rise of "gated" communities, as people fence themselves and their children in, something which only foreign diplomats and Party officials did in the past.

HOUSING

With the rapid demolition of many of the traditional courtyard homes that made cities like Beijing so attractive in the past, most Chinese now live in high-rise apartment blocks. The PRC has severe housing

problems, despite a massive amount of construction.
Limited space means homes often look cluttered, with
every inch of space used for storage. The per capita
living space in most major cities is only 76.4 square
feet (7.1 sq. m). People live on top of each other with
little privacy. Conflicts are common over minor
issues—a playful child, a noisy radio. House prices
are high and many will never be able to afford their
dream home.

In the countryside, farming families tend to own
their homes, and whenever they have some spare
cash, they build another room, or a whole new
storey. But as more young people get married and
enjoy the freedom to move around the country, the
traditional extended family is starting to break up,
and in the cities three or even four generations all
living under one roof is becoming less common.

SOCIAL RELATIONS AND OCCUPATIONS

Many Chinese now are graduates, but finding a suitable job is not easy. More jobs now are awarded on merit and advertised openly, rather than just assigned to graduates by the universities; but good *guanxi* still matters when young people are job hunting. The days of state-run "work units," or *danwei*, which provided everything for their employees and their families, from marriage partners to housing, schools to hospital care, are long gone, and when the recession started and China's economy slowed down, many workers realized belatedly that they had no job security.

DAILY LIFE

The Chinese rise early, around 6:00 a.m., and are often at work or school by 7:15 a.m. The journey to work in big cities is hard, as all roads and all forms of transport are packed and standing in line is unheard of. From childhood onward, at school and at work, many people have a short rest (*xiu xi*) after lunch and find it hard to function if they do not get the chance to rest. In the days of Mao, paid holidays were almost unknown, but nowadays most people have time off during Chinese New Year, on May 1, and on National Day (October 1).

People finish work or school around 6:00 p.m and buy food for the evening meal on the way home, from supermarkets or street markets, which stay open very late, seven days a week. Either men or women may do the cooking at home; boys and girls learn to cook from childhood, seemingly enjoying

cooking almost as much as eating the finished results. People go out to eat quite often, as prices in restaurants or roadside stalls are reasonable.

EDUCATION

The school year begins in September; students have their winter holidays from mid-January to the end of February, their summer holidays from mid-July to the end of August. Their lives are much more regulated than in the West, with even very young children having responsibilities such as classroom monitor or helping with the cleaning; these duties are taken very seriously. Children often stay late at school with their teachers on the spot to help with homework, of which they have a huge amount. This regime continues with highly competitive exams up to university entrance. Discipline is strict, with much rote learning. Class sizes are big: up to eighty children or more is not unusual in rural areas.

This extract (complete with original English mistakes) comes from a blog run by Kaiser Kuo, who works for Baidu.com, the Chinese equivalent of

Google. Written by a thirteen-year-old Chinese girl, her heartfelt words could be echoed by millions of other high-school students: "I am a junior student in high school. Be a student isn't easy in China, I need wake up at 6:00 at morning. The first class begins at 7:15 am, and the last class is ending at 7:00 pm, of course we have two hours rest when after lunch. Every teachers and parents wants us can go to good school finally. We learn 9 subjects, additional these subjects are very difficult. We never do experiment in physics, biology and chemistry class, my teacher don't have time . . . . I usually finished my homework at 0:00 am or later, most of Chinese students study until 2:00 am for getting a good grades."

Parents are, mostly, fiercely supportive of schools; teachers and parents often speak on the phone to discuss their children's results or behavior, even at university level. This means parents (almost everyone after their late twenties) spend a lot of time pushing their children, as well as working hard themselves, saving to put their child through university, perhaps to buy a house, maybe even to travel abroad.

Another comment on Kaiser Kuo's site gives a thirty-something worker's rather disillusioned point of view of his daily grind:

"The improvement of life quality in China was pretty obvious up to mid-2000s. Young people's most coveted jobs changed from global company positions to state-owned enterprise and Internet company jobs. But . . . people are not well-off compared to the world standard. Workplace competition is fierce and many people do not follow rules or etiquette. They do not have the least respect for co-workers or have a slightest idea of what ethic code means. People's earnings keep increasing, but life happiness is not."

THE THIRD AGE

At least one sector of the population have a rather less stressful life—older people can relax, help look after their grandchildren, go to the park to dance, sing, or do *taijiquan*, travel, and know that they are respected and loved by their families. Chinese people are living

longer, healthier lives; this is the main reason why the One Child policy has been officially abandoned, as more youngsters are needed to pay their pensions.

LOVE AND MARRIAGE, OR NOT

The parents of today's young Chinese men and women had to get the permission of their superiors in their *danweis* (work units) to get engaged, married, or divorced. This was in part an attempt to stop the forced early marriages of old China; the minimum age for getting married, or even dating, was set at around twenty-five, which was also a way of controlling population. Things are freer now and it is more common to live together before marriage; the problem for young couples (as in the West) is a shortage of affordable accommodation.

In the past, a happy marriage was rare; the husband's mother was often cruel to the new bride, who rarely left the house. Widows did not remarry, as it was thought immoral to marry more than once. Since 1949, women's legal position has improved considerably: however, the equality pendulum is swinging back, to the surprise and alarm of feminists. The derogatory phrase "leftover women" has been coined by the Party to describe Chinese women who are still unmarried at the ripe old age of twenty-seven. According to a book on the topic by American academic Leta Hong Fincher, in 2011 China's official Xinhua news agency published an editorial saying that: "The tragedy is women don't realize that as they age they are worth less . . . , so by the time they get their MA or PhD, they are already old, like yellowed pearls." Dr. Hong Fincher writes: "The government believes that society is more stable with fewer single people; new families drive consumption and the property boom. Plus, if educated females are married, then 'better quality' children will be born." Despite the official revival of this age-old social stigma, today's highly educated women are no longer easy to browbeat, and are fighting back. Some have taken a different word, similar to "leftover" in Chinese, but which means "triumphant," and are using it to describe themselves and their decision to stay single.

When women do marry, they no longer feel obliged to stay that way. Numbers of divorces have grown every year since 2003, when divorce was made simpler and cheaper. In Beijing, 40 percent of marriages now end in divorce, according to the Chinese Web site Weibo. The reasons given include: social media, making love affairs easy, and the fact that women expect more of their lives now,

and will no longer put up with domestic violence or unhappiness; also, they can earn as much or more in a job than men, so no longer need a husband to pay the bills. The stigma of divorce has gone—and, surprisingly for bureaucratic China, divorce costs just a few RMB, plus about half an hour to fill in the form. As always, things are much more traditional in the rural areas.

chapter six

TIME OUT

Go out into the streets at first light in any city in China and you will find row upon row of people silently absorbed in their morning exercises, each going through the series of movements that make up the slow, intricate ballet of *qigong*. *Qi* means life force and *qigong* is a series of exercises—combining movement, breathing, and visualization—that direct the flow of energy around the body. Some take it to the point where they try to perform what are almost circus tricks, such as driving nails through boards with their bare hands. Others practice *qigong* to heal illness by a "laying on of hands." The streets are home to many such

activities, which tend to be done collectively; solitude is generally avoided. Ballroom dancing, singing in the public parks, running, and people-watching are all done in large crowds, in the open air, and cost nothing.

The Chinese are careful with their money, but increased leisure time and more spare cash mean that pursuits such as eating out, playing and watching sports such as badminton, ping pong, basketball and football, taking part in martial arts, stamp collecting, keeping pet birds, reading, playing *mah-jong* and chess (very noisily), going to clubs and karaoke bars, watching TV, going to the cinema and concerts, shopping and social media are all enjoyed in the cities (there are fewer facilities and less spare time and money in rural areas). As a visitor, all of these pastimes are open to you, too, as participant or spectator. All the major cities have English-language Web sites giving information on what's on locally, and Chinese friends, colleagues, and tour guides will be happy to tell you more, or accompany you.

Chinese tourism is also increasing year on year: those who cannot afford to go overseas enjoy traveling in their own vast country; in October 2015, *China Daily* reported that the number of Chinese tourists enjoying "staycations" is predicted to rise to 750 million. Many Chinese tourists do go overseas—mostly to Asia, but the number going to Europe, Australia, and the USA is booming.

PARKS
Parks are wonderful places, the very essence of the collective spirit that is still so much a part of China.

They are much more stylized than the open green spaces that Westerners are used to, with far fewer trees and more pavilions and rocks. There is often a small entrance fee, and many retired people stay all day in the park chatting, giving their caged birds an airing, playing music from Peking Operas, or singing old songs. Small children run around in the play areas by day; in the evening, courting couples find rare privacy in the darker corners of the parks, as the older people and babies wend their way home.

SPORTS
You can follow any sport in China as a player or a spectator. Talking about sport is a good ice breaker: most Chinese men and women are interested in sports, especially those in which China excels such as basketball, swimming, athletics, gymnastics, and badminton. The most popular sports are those that do not need expensive equipment, so although skiing,

golf, and tennis are increasingly enjoyed, far more people practice sports such as basketball (about 300 million play regularly) or ping pong. When the Beijing Olympics took place in 2008, millions volunteered to help the many visitors, some learning English specially, and China led the gold medal count.

Celebrity

One of the most famous Chinese sportsmen is Yao Ming, a basketball player who started playing for the Shanghai Sharks as a teenager and then finally played with the Houston Rockets. The only child of two basketball players, he stands 7 foot 6 inches (2.29 meters) high and weighed 11 pounds (5 kilos) when he was born. After injuries forced him to retire in 2011, he became an ambassador for endangered wildlife and donated much of the money he had made as a player to that cause, and to helping his old club, the Shanghai Sharks.

EATING IN AND OUT

Long before the West woke up to the benefits of healthy eating, the Chinese had worked out a complex system of diet that they believed contributes to wellbeing. The traditional Chinese diet has many vegetables, with food cooked fast so that the goodness is not destroyed. Shopping for food is done with gusto and everything is prodded, shaken, sniffed, and thoroughly examined before being purchased. Few Chinese eat "ready meals"; food is freshly cooked for each meal, and fish, meat, and poultry are often killed only a short time before they are cooked. In restaurants you often choose your fish from a selection swimming in a huge tank.

A fantastic range of different foods is on offer, some delicious, such as dumplings, sweet and

sour soup, and Mongolian hotpot, some less to Western tastes, such as hundred-year-old eggs, sea cucumbers, salted eels, or donkey stew. If you are overwhelmed by a desire for familiar food, fast-food outlets sell hamburgers and pizzas; there are Italian, Indian, Japanese, Korean, and Mexican restaurants, and supermarkets (the French chain Carrefour arrived first, but others have followed) that sell the foods of which, in the past, homesick Westerners could only dream—bread, cheese, milk, coffee, and real chocolate. Young urban Chinese now happily drink takeaway Starbucks while munching on a pizza slice—but they are still proud of their cuisine and love to introduce foreign visitors to it.

In many restaurants, bars, and clubs in today's China, you could be anywhere in the modern world; venues are fashionably sleek, quiet, and clean. Out in the real world, however, and even sometimes at banquets, things are a bit more down to earth. Noisy eating and loud slurping is omnipresent, especially in backstreet restaurants where migrant workers eat; but there is usually so much ambient noise anyway that you will probably remain mercifully unaware of it. In many cities, especially in the north, coal dust and fine sand blowing in from the Gobi Desert, combined with smoking low-quality cigarettes, cause people to indulge in loud throat clearing and long-distance spitting. Decades of attempts to stop this horrible habit have had limited success; public spittoons are still found in cheaper restaurants and are well used by the clientele. It may help you tolerate it if you reflect on the working conditions of many people's lives—laboring for hours on building sites, with little or no protection, breathing in quantities of dust is unavoidable.

Restaurant Etiquette

When you arrive at the more upmarket restaurants, staff will rush forward and guide you to a table. Do not worry if you cannot read Chinese; even if the menu is not in English, it should have pictures of the main dishes, or you can always point to what someone else is eating. The staff will be very attentive and will pour out tea, arrange a clean linen napkin on your lap as though you were a child, show you how to use chopsticks, and generally fuss over you. This can be quite embarrassing for Westerners, but it is meant to be polite, so just smile and say thank you (and leave a tip with the bill). Fast-food joints have no truck with such niceties and are just like anywhere else in the world, only more crowded.

TIPPING

The Chinese do not usually tip. For foreign visitors, in restaurants a 10 percent tip is normal. In upmarket hotels it is usual to tip the bellboy and other staff, but not in backpackers' hotels. Chinese taxi drivers will accept a tip, but will not expect one. If you are allocated a driver by the organization looking after you, he will be pleased if you offer cigarettes.

REGIONAL CUISINE

Chinese local dishes are said to belong to four, or eight, or ten culinary schools, depending on whom you believe. Canton, Shandong, Sichuan, and Yangzhou make up four: Hunan, Fujian, Anhui, and Zhejiang make eight; include Beijing and Shanghai and you have ten. You could also add the Middle Eastern influenced cooking of the Hui and Uighur people, whose roadside stalls produce wonderful (and cheap) lamb kebabs wrapped in naan bread, served with salad and hot spicy sauce.

Cantonese Food

Cantonese cuisine has a wide range of ingredients; there is a Chinese saying that "The Cantonese will eat

anything with wings, except a plane, and anything with four legs, except a table." River and seafood are widely used, as well as birds, rats, and insects. Some of the more esoteric dishes are "three kinds of snake stewed," cat meat, stewed mountain turtle, and crispy skin suckling pig.

Shandong Food

Shandong lies on a peninsula, so its cuisine is dominated by seafood. Dishes include stewed sea cucumber with scallion, stewed snakehead eggs, and sea slugs with crab ovum.

Sichuan Food

Sichuan cuisine is renowned for its hot, peppery flavor. The Sichuanese use a special black pepper that leaves the lips numb—not unpleasant when one grows accustomed to it. The variety of tastes is summed up in the phrase "a hundred dishes with a hundred flavors." Dishes include shredded pork with fish flavor, stewed bean curd with minced pork in pepper sauce, and dry-roast rock carp.

Huaiyang Food

Huaiyang cuisine integrates the best of dishes in Yangzhou, Zhenjiang, Huaian, and other places south of the Yangtze River, stressing "freshness and tenderness, careful preparation, cutting skill, bright color, beautiful arrangements, and delicate flavoring" according to one enthusiast. Famous dishes include beggar's chicken, fried mandarin fish with sweet and sour sauce, and minced pork balls in a casserole.

Vegetable Dishes

Vegetable dishes have been popular since the Song dynasty (960–1279). They were divided into three schools: Monastery Vegetable Dishes, Court Vegetable Dishes, and Folk Vegetable Dishes. Ingredients include green leaved vegetables, fruit, edible mushrooms, and bean curd cooked in vegetable oil, which, according to one Chinese cookery writer, are "delicious in taste, rich in nutrition, easy to digest, and may help prevent cancer."

TRADITONAL DRINKS: GREEN TEA AND HOT RICE WINE

The Chinese drink large quantities of green tea, without milk or sugar. Tea is drunk constantly at meetings, at work, in restaurants, and at formal meals. It is usually served in mugs with lids to keep it warm. Teabags and tea strainers are not used, and drinking tea without swallowing a mouthful of soggy tea leaves requires concentration: try using the lid as a strainer when sipping.

Tea is divided into green, black, perfumed, white, and Wulong tea. Some of the most sought after green teas are Long jing and Bi luo chun; among black teas, Qi hong and Yun feng are special. National appreciation of good tea is on a par with the innate

knowledge French people have of good wine, and taken equally seriously. The Chinese often give small beautifully decorated tea caddies containing special teas as a gift.

On cold days try yellow rice wine, served hot in little porcelain cups and tasting rather like sherry. More lethal is *maotai*, the Chinese answer to vodka; there are also many light Chinese beers, as well as a growing range of good Chinese wines, some produced in partnership with French wine producers. Soft drinks are available everywhere, and fruit juices made from tropical fruits grown in the south of China are delicious.

COFFEE SHOPS AND TEAHOUSES
As well as the growing numbers of coffee shops, the last twenty years has seen the reemergence of traditional teahouses. For centuries the haunt of intellectuals and literati, who would while away their days discussing philosophy or writing poetry, they are

located in quiet places in beautiful surroundings, and offer that rare commodity in perennially noisy China— tranquillity. The quiet is broken only by leisurely music played on the *zheng*, a stringed instrument similar to a zither. The teahouse even spawned its own TV series, a China/UK coproduction called *Joy Luck Street*. Centered around the comings and goings in a teahouse, it was inspired by the long-running British TV soap *Coronation Street*, whose central location is a (much less refined) English pub.

SMOKERS' PARADISE

Cigarette smoking is widespread among men in China, less so among women. In the past it was very hard to escape from other people's cigarette smoke in restaurants. Young Chinese men set on having a good night out balanced a lit cigarette in one hand, a pair of chopsticks and a glass in the other— managing to smoke, drink, eat, shout, and gesticulate all at the same time. Smoking is now banned indoors and in cars.

SHOPPING FOR PLEASURE

From roadside stalls to giant shopping malls, from
night markets to entire streets specializing in one exotic
product such as pearls, silk flowers, or jade, modern
China is a shopper's paradise. As Sunday was never
a religious holiday in China, and as labor is cheap,
shops are open seven days a week, from about nine in
the morning to nine at night, sometimes later; when
Chinese tourists come to Europe, they complain about
the limited opening hours of the shops they have come
so far to patronize. For the Chinese, shopping is both a
pleasure and their patriotic duty, as it keeps the wheels
of the economy turning.

In theory, shop prices are fixed, but there is often
room for a bit of haggling. In the markets prices
start at about three times the eventual price you can
expect to pay. Many of the traders are astute young
saleswomen, with a few token salesmen as well.
They are very insistent and often know not only
English, but also some Russian, French, and German.
As China manufactures almost everything sold in
Western shops, you can shop till you drop—and then
buy an extra suitcase to bring it all home.

Fake Goods

Almost everything with a logo is probably a fake; be
especially wary of pirated CDs, DVDs, and computer
software that may not work and will probably damage
your device. If you are offered anything "antique," it
will either be a replica or else it is being offered for
sale illegally. Genuine (you hope) antiques can only
be bought at official stores, and will bear a special
seal authorizing their export. China has lost enough

antiquities through war and conflict in the past, and is hanging on to what it has left. You may find some legitimately available antiques in Hong Kong, where they were taken by families fleeing the turmoil of the 1930s and '40s.

What To Buy

Apart from hi-tech products such as smartphones and computers, China is also rich in carving, embroidery, pottery and porcelain, glassware, weaving, printing, wood carving, and dyeing, and perfect replicas of ancient cultural relics. Folk art such as patchwork makes a good gift to take home.

CHANGING MONEY

All cash transactions are in renminbi ("the people's currency")—also known as the yuan (dollar), a denomination of the renminbi currency—which is what you will be given when you change your money at the airport or at banks or hotels. There are 1, 5, 10, 20,

50, and 100 yuan notes. The renminbi (RMB) is broken down into 100 fen, and there are coins of 1, 2, 5, and 10. To complicate matters, the Chinese always refer to the 10 fen coin as either a "jiao" or a "mao."

Exchange rates are much the same everywhere and there are branches of most Western banks in the big cities, or you can change money in the Bank of China, or your hotel. China is inching toward the day when the RMB becomes fully convertible; in the meantime, keep receipts as proof that your RMB were obtained legally, to ensure that you can change the local currency back when you leave the country.

CARRY CASH
Credit and debit cards, although used increasingly, are not yet universally accepted, so you need to carry more cash than normal. Crime in China is low, and many visitors feel safer than in New York or London: nonetheless, watch out for pickpockets.

NIGHTLIFE AND CULTURE
Big cities in China used to heave a collective sigh and settle down wearily for the night around 9:00 p.m. There were few street lamps and fewer advertising signs to light up the night sky; the handful of dreary state-run restaurants closed at 8:00 p.m., or earlier if they ran out of food. Now the cities never sleep and a vast range of cinemas, restaurants, clubs, and bars to suit all tastes and budgets mean you need never be bored.

MUSIC

The love of music goes back thousands of years in China. Bamboo pipes tuned to resemble birdsong are thought to have been the earliest instruments played. Confucius believed music to be a vital part of culture, and over succeeding dynasties Chinese musicians developed many different instruments, some such as the *guzheng*, unique to China, others such as the *pipa* coming from other parts of Asia. European music made its first known appearance in 1601, when the Italian Jesuit Matteo Ricci brought a harpsichord to the Ming court and trained four eunuchs to play it. Nowadays, traditional and modern Chinese and all forms of Western music happily coexist.

Chinese Opera

This form of traditional drama involves acrobatics, fencing, and boxing, as well as music and singing. Singers wear elaborate costumes and highly stylized makeup; their audience (mostly older people) know the story by heart, so frequently get up and walk about during the performance, crunch noisily on snacks, and generally behave quite differently from the

quasi-religious silence of opera audiences in the West. For Westerners, the sound harks romantically (if discordantly) back to ancient China; but young Chinese much prefer pop music.

Chinese Classical Music

The most atmospheric place to hear this is in teahouses, though concerts also take place in the big cities now that this type of music has been revived. Players often wear Tang dynasty dress; famous poems are set to music, sung in a thin falsetto voice, with eloquent pauses a part of the performance. It is not easy listening, and without financial support from the state would probably die out, but it is worth hearing.

Western Classical Music

The tradition of hard work, fierce competition, and perfectionism means that China produces many fine classical musicians, such as the world renowned pianist Lang Lang. If you have a chance, go to a concert in one of China's stunning new concert halls, at much lower prices than you would pay in the West.

Revolutionary Songs

During the Cultural Revolution, these songs were the only ones allowed and for a while songs such as "The East Is Red" came to define mainland Chinese music. The only place you are likely to hear them today is on souvenir electronic cigarette lighters emblazoned with Mao's face, and, much more pleasingly, in the parks, where older folk sing them with gusto, having apparently forgotten the suffering they endured when singing these songs was mandatory. That said, some of these old songs are very melodic.

Modern Music: Pop, Rock, and Rap
Chinese pop, rap, and rock music, some home grown, some from Taiwan and Hong Kong, is growing in popularity, and the Internet gives young Chinese easy access to foreign bands. China now has its own rock festival called the Midi Modern Music Festival, which attracts about 80,000 visitors and has been held in Beijing, Shanghai, and Shenzhen every year since 1997. Both foreign and Chinese bands play there, and the festival also tries to raise awareness of environmental issues.

ART
Classical Art Before 1949
Chinese painting is arguably the oldest continuous artistic tradition in the world, quite unlike any Western style of painting. Artists and calligraphers used brushes dipped in black ink or colored pigments, applying them rapidly to paper or silk. There are many subjects: landscapes featuring mountains, rivers, and rocks, scenes of court life, or animals. One of the most famous is *Riverside Scene during Qingming*, painted by Zhang Zeduan during the Song dynasty. It is on a scroll about 18 feet long and 10 inches wide (5.5 m by 25 cm), and shows in fascinating detail the daily life of residents of the city, rich and poor, with detailed images of streets, houses,

boats, bridges, market places, and scenery. There are over 800 people pictured, each in different clothes. Go and see it in the Palace Museum in Beijing; the colors are still fresh and bright, partly because these types of scrolls were kept rolled up and only opened on special occasions.

Art After 1949
From 1949 onward, artists were told to imitate the Soviet Union's style of socialist realism and some were tasked with churning out the same pictures, for example of happy peasants gathered around Mao, again and again. In the late 1950s, giant outdoor murals of naïve peasant art showing (idealized) rural life became popular. Many priceless works of art—no

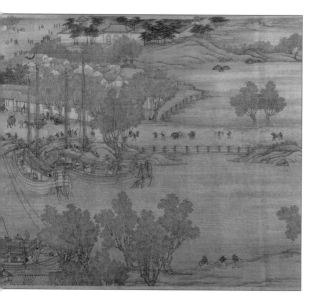

one knows how many—were deliberately destroyed by the Red Guards during the Cultural Revolution as part of Mao's campaign against the "Four Olds" (old customs, old culture, old habits, old ideas).

Nowadays artists feel freer to innovate, but they still have to watch their step. Artist Ai Wei Wei has become known worldwide for his original work, but his fierce criticism of the government has frequently landed him in serious trouble. As with religion, the government will only allow people to go so far.

There are many museums around China showing classical and modern art, and shops sell beautifully detailed copies of traditional paintings. Chinese art, old and new, has been achieving record prices at auctions.

A FEW "MUST SEES"

Here are a few, chosen from hundreds, of the wonderful sights that this diverse land has to offer.

The Great Wall

Built over the course of thirteen dynasties, the Great Wall—in fact, many walls—is reckoned to have been 13,000 miles (20,921 km) long, though two-thirds have now vanished. The remains of the wall stretch about 4,000 miles (6,437 km) across the bleak plains of northern China; its western end is at Jiayuguan Pass, or "First and Greatest Pass Under Heaven," some 932 miles (1,500 km) from Beijing, in the arid deserts of Gansu province. The easiest way to see it is to take a day trip from Beijing.

The Forbidden City

Just off Tiananmen (Gate of Heavenly Peace) Square, in the heart of Beijing, the Forbidden City is somewhere to go early in the morning when it is still quiet—and then stay all day, as it contains

nearly 1,000 buildings and served as the home of the Chinese emperors for five hundred years. It has 14 million visitors a year and is a UNESCO World Heritage Site.

The Terracotta Warriors

In 1974, farmers near Xi'an—568 miles (914 km)
northwest of Beijing—were digging a well when they
stumbled across a collection of life-size soldiers,
chariots, and horses. They had been buried with
Emperor Qin Shi Huang in 209 BCE, to protect him in
the afterlife. There are over 8,000 of them, and around
670 horses; they had been beautifully painted, but the
paints did not survive exposure to the air.

Shanghai Waterfront

Also known as the Bund (the Persian/Hindi word for
an embankment), the waterfront of Shanghai faces
the most spectacularly modern part of Pudong (as
seen in the film *Spectre*) across the Huangpu River,
and is backed by historical buildings from the 1870s
to the 1930s that once housed banks and trading
houses from around the world. Barges and passenger
boats from all over China pass by on the busy river;
at night their foghorns ring out across the water.

Guilin

A boat trip along the Li River from the ancient
southern town of Guilin takes you past rock
formations and twisted pine trees that bring
traditional Chinese paintings alive. Many ethnic
minorities live in this part of China, adding to
the color of the area.

Tibet

You will need a special visa to visit Tibet, but it is
worth the effort and money to see Lhasa (in Tibetan,
"The Land of the Gods"), with the Potala Palace
where the Dalai Lama lived, the Drepung Monastery,
and many other temples, as well as discovering
the deeply spiritual Buddhist culture of the
Tibetan people, very different from the pragmatic
materialism of the rest of China.

The Silk Road

The Silk Road was a trade route from China to the Mediterranean for over 2,000 years. You can follow it from Xi'an across the Gobi Desert by train, and visit the oasis of Dunhuang, Urumqi, the capital of Xinjiang where the Uyghur people live, and Kashgar, last stop before the Russian border.

Lijiang

An old town situated in Yunnan province in the far south of China, Lijiang is the home of the indigenous Naxi people. Its maze of winding cobbled streets has become a destination for young Chinese artists and is full of lively clubs and small, reasonably priced restaurants. Nearby is Jade Dragon Mountain, a green, subtropical paradise that is a relief after the dry dusty north. Lijiang is yet another UNESCO World Heritage site. China has forty-eight of them, second only to Italy.

chapter seven

TRAVEL, HEALTH, & SAFETY

TRAVEL

The importance of moving goods and people has always been taken seriously by China's rulers. In the fifth century BCE the Chinese starting building the Grand Canal from Beijing to Hangzhou—at 1,104 miles (1,176 km) it is still the longest in the world. By the tenth century they had worked out a system of locks to cope with differing heights of the land. In the past decades, China has poured money into its transport infrastructure, and while traveling in China is not always easy because of the huge numbers of people trying to do the same thing, its modern airports, trains, railways stations, and roads are impressive.

Safety records for trains, buses, and planes are fairly good and tickets are affordable. The hardest thing can be buying the ticket—crowds outside ticket offices in bus and train stations behave like a vast, vicious football scrum, and for once being foreign is no help at all. You can now buy tickets in advance online for planes, trains, and buses, or use a travel agent. Unless you are a masochist, do not travel at national holiday periods.

Travel is relatively safe in China, alone or in a group. People may stare at you, but are unlikely to rob or molest you; if you ask for help you will get it, but otherwise people will tend to leave you in peace. There will usually be someone kind and helpful, perhaps a student, teacher, or business person, who will make it their job to adopt you temporarily, perhaps to practice their English or simply to make sure you are OK.

GETTING ABOUT TOWN
On Foot
Walking around towns can be difficult, due to the volume of people and traffic, but is never dull. Streets in China are packed with pedestrians, peddlers of everything from socks to pirated CDs to cell phone paraphernalia. Tiny homemade stalls offer food, bike or car repairs; tumbledown shacks housing family-run shops huddle in the shadow of huge designer outlets. The interest you feel in people watching will be reciprocated many times over by out-of-towners, who will stare openly at your round eyes, funny hair, large

nose, and differently shaped body. But their attention is not hostile, and a friendly "*Ni hao*" (Hello) will be greeted with delight.

Walks in the countryside are best in the southwest, where there are mountains and bamboo forests to wander through; footpaths are marked and there are old Buddhist monasteries and ancient wayside inns to stay in.

Wheels

Thirty years ago, Chinese cities resounded to the ringing of bicycle bells as the entire population cycled to work or school; nowadays the background music is provided by millions of internal combustion engines and of motor horns sounded in cacophonous frustration. Car ownership in China has soared as people become wealthier. Chinese figures put the number of private cars at 154 million at the start of 2015; cars now outnumber motorcycles on China's busy roads. Motorbikes, often carrying entire families,

still comprise about 40 percent of privately owned vehicles, but are now banned in many city centers: they are considered noisy, polluting, and dangerous, and have too often been used to rob passers-by.

In poorer areas, people are still dependent on bicycles, tricycles, and antique tractors, often towing homemade trailers, and loaded (or overloaded) to gravity defying heights. They are used to transport everything from relatives who need to get to hospital, to farm animals, to precariously balanced piles of goods destined for sale in some faraway market.

You can hire bicycles and there are cycling lanes in many towns. Motorbikes and cars can also be rented, but are not for the fainthearted.

If you are offered a ride in a rickshaw in a big city, you are probably taking your life in your hands if you agree; plus, it may cost more than a normal taxi, as it is not usually metered. Outside the cities it is a pleasant way to travel though, but agree the fare in advance.

The pollution levels in China are so bad that many older vehicles have been compulsorily scrapped and lie rusting in enormous scrapyards. China is moving slowly toward using home produced electric cars to reduce pollution levels. Perhaps, as pollution increases and levels of public fitness fall, the government may start to encourage the use of bicycles again in big cities, as has happened in London, Paris and other congested places.

Public Transport

Beijing and Shanghai both have excellent metro systems, which are user-friendly, cheap, quick, and reliable.

Urban buses are very cheap but also very crowded. In the big cities they tend to be modern and well equipped, with screens and electronic maps telling you (in English) where your stop is. Getting on is hard, and getting off can be harder, but people will make way for you and smile if you try and say "Excuse me" in Chinese, or even English.

Taxis

The taxi service is good, and taxis are easily hailed in the streets. They are strictly metered, though make sure that the driver starts the meter running. Few taxi drivers speak English, so it is advisable to get someone to write down your destination in Chinese and show it to the driver. Driving in towns can be nerve-racking, especially if you are sitting in the front seat. Tipping used to be forbidden and is not expected (see page 102).

Disabled Access

Facilities for disabled visitors are still not good, but attitudes toward those with disabilities are improving. Deng Pufang, one of the sons of Deng Xiaoping, was confined to a wheelchair after he "fell" from a window during the bitter power struggles of the Cultural Revolution. He devoted the rest of his life to campaigning for people with disabilities. There is still a long way to go; access to public transport is hard, and some streets resemble an obstacle race, with uneven sidewalks and no ramps. Disabled toilet facilities are rare. There are plenty of Web sites for travelers with disabilities to consult before departure.

The Human Touch
Lack of official provision for people with disabilities can bring out the kindness of strangers. One blind American visitor to the Forbidden City was given a personal tour by the guide, who removed the ropes separating the exhibits from the crowds and steered the man's hand over the items, while describing them all in flawless English.

INTERCITY
Air Travel
The Chinese used to have a poor record on air safety for domestic flights, but this has improved. The air network is extensive and airports are regularly upgraded. Buying air tickets online (on English-language Web sites) is straightforward and increased competition means there are some good deals to be found.

Rail Travel
China's modern trains are punctual, clean, and comfortable. There are "soft" and "hard" seats and sleepers, the hard class much cheaper but overcrowded and uncomfortable. Your ticket is good for one train only, so do not miss it! Older trains are still in service, though most steam trains have been retired to the China Railway Museum just outside Beijing.

A Word to the Wise

Since smoking in public was banned, non-smokers no longer have to inhale the smoke from cheap cigarettes that Chinese men once smoked incessantly on long train journeys. However, if you travel by hard sleeper, you still have to listen to them all snoring in concert as six berths are stacked close together. If you value your sleep, take some earplugs.

Bus Travel

Long-distance bus travel has improved considerably. Tickets can be bought online or via agencies and are numbered. There are on-board videos and music, but rarely an on-board toilet and pit stops are few and far between. But there are advantages to bus travel: as novelist and long-term China resident, Nicholas Richards, wrote in *The China Dispatch* in 2011: "Bus travel . . . offers a gorgeous, leisurely ride . . . a taste of

China that few other foreigners get to experience. Huge windows revealing luscious views of village life are just an arm's reach away, giving access to places that trains and planes wouldn't . . . take you, like the grasslands of rural Sichuan, or the mushroom fields of Yunnan. Best of all, you're sure to be the only *waiguoren* [foreigner] in sight."

Be Prepared
Public toilets used to be unspeakable; they are a lot better now in towns and busy tourist venues, but in rural areas they can be primitive beyond belief. Do not be surprised if going to the toilet is a communal experience, with no doors to provide privacy. Take your own toilet paper and a damp towel/wet wipes to be able to clean your hands, as there is rarely any running water to enable you to do so.

Travel by Boat
From four-day luxury cruises up the Yangtze River to short ferry hops with the locals around Hainan Island, Hong Kong, or Shanghai, China offers lovers of boat trips plenty of opportunity. There are many good private travel agencies who can help you find out more—ferry companies are not yet as up-to-speed as airlines and trains when it comes to English-language Web sites.

RULES AND REGULATIONS
Visas
Individual travelers can obtain a thirty-day tourist visa at any Chinese consulate or other organization

authorized by the Ministry of Foreign Affairs. Visitors wanting to stay beyond thirty days can usually gain an extension (up to sixty days) by applying to the local Public Security Bureau. The extension must be obtained prior to the expiry of the existing visa.

Business travelers require an invitation letter from a Chinese organization or enterprise to obtain a visa. Some enter on a tourist visa, but this can lead to problems. You may wish to leave all the arrangements in the hands of an agency such as China Travel Service.

Tibet

Tourists need to obtain entry permits from the Tibet Tourism Administration or one of its overseas offices. Try to travel there overland: if you fly in, you risk the fate of an American journalist who spent three days of his four-day Tibet visa (which he had waited months to obtain) in bed, recovering from severe altitude sickness. The body takes time to acclimatize to the thinner air of Lhasa, which is 11,975 feet (3,650 m) above sea level.

Staying Within the Law

Holders of tourist visas must pass through Chinese ports of entry designated as open to visitors from abroad. Some places, particularly in border areas, are restricted, and travelers have been arrested, even expelled, for straying into these zones. Foreigners visiting China on normal travel permits should not engage in activities that do not comply with their visa, such as taking up employment, study, or reporting; the authorities are particularly sensitive about journalists masquerading as tourists.

Taking Photos

The Chinese have become "selfie" fanatics, so foreign visitors snapping away in front of tourist sites just blend into the crowd. But do not point your camera at soldiers guarding government buildings, and be careful about taking pictures at airports or anywhere that might be considered "strategic," such as a dockyard or border post. Photos of high-speed trains and railway stations will probably be safe enough. Foreign visitors longing to photograph the few remaining Chinese steam trains had better be quick, as they are likely to be retired soon—unlamented by the unsentimental locals.

HEALTH

China's health care model is similar to that of the USA, in that people must either pay for treatment or purchase health insurance, topped up by the state. The best medical care is available in large cities, where privately run hospitals are the best, but can often cost up to ten times more than a public hospital. China has been trying to address the growing disparity between rural and urban medical provision, and since 2005 around 800 million rural residents have been given basic medical cover, with about half of their costs covered by the government; around 95 percent of the total population now has basic health insurance. In rural areas, health care is rudimentary, with poorly trained medical personnel and little equipment or medication, though some areas have better quality care than others.

VACCINATIONS

Few are needed, but China does have a high incidence of hepatitis-B, with about one-third of the world's infections occurring there. In some areas inoculations against Japanese encephalitis are recommended. Rabies is present outside the big cities but rare in urban areas. Check online to see the full list, and get vaccinations done about two months before you go, as some take time to provide immunity.

If you become ill in China, take a taxi to the nearest public hospital (its address will be online in English) and ask to be treated in the so-called VIP wards, or *gaogan bingfang*. Most VIP wards provide medical services to foreigners and have English-speaking doctors and nurses. VIP wards charge higher prices but are still cheap by Western standards. Dental care, cosmetic surgery, and other services are widely available in urban areas, though costs and quality vary.

Traditional Medicine

Traditional Chinese medicine (TCM) is based on the understanding that the body is a cosmos in miniature, and that illness is a reflection of disharmony in the flow of *qi* (vital energy) through the organism. Acupuncture seeks to correct the flow of *qi*; it involves the insertion

of thin stainless steel needles into energy points of the body, connecting the needles to an electric current, and then setting them to vibrate several hundred times a minute. The traditional system worked, partly because everyone believed in it, partly because there was little alternative. Although medicine in China is increasingly westernized, TCM is still widely used, and there are Chinese medicine hospitals located throughout the country.

HYGIENE AND PERSONAL SAFETY

When traveling take your own chopsticks, cutlery, and cup, to be sure that you do not catch hepatitis-B from insanitary ones. Chinese food is cooked fast, at high temperatures, and on the spot, so food poisoning is mercifully rare, but the use of dirty utensils, possibly washed in unclean water, is a risk. Road traffic accidents are an increasing hazard, and you should also check fire exits, which are frequently locked to keep out robbers.

HOPE FOR THE BEST; PREPARE FOR THE WORST

- Some prescription medicines sold are fake, poorly stored, or out of date, so take with you a supply of any medicines you may need.
- Hypodermic needles are often used more than once, so take some unused sterile needles with you in case you need an injection.
- Take a spare pair of glasses, and your prescription.
- Keep all documentation related to any medical expenses you incur.
- Don't even think about going to China without adequate travel insurance.

Petty crime has increased, and you should be as careful as you would be at home, especially at night. Foreigners are seen as walking ATMs, so watch your money and your cell phone. There are also increasing numbers of scams, such as the one where beautiful young women in the streets of Beijing and Shanghai ask gullible foreign men to take their photos, then invite them along to local bars for a drink and vanish, leaving the men with a huge bill or even the threat of violence. That said, violent crime against foreigners is rare and most Chinese will regard you as a guest in their country and take personal responsibility for your safety. If something does go wrong, report it to the nearest police station which will issue a "confirmation of loss" report. Your embassy can help in case of serious accidents, or the sudden death of a family member or friend.

chapter eight

BUSINESS BRIEFING

Few tourists visit the Zhejiang Merchants Museum, set in the beautiful old town of Hangzhou, southeast of Shanghai. If they did, they would see an exhibition of portraits of twenty-first century local heroes: not soldiers, scientists, or revolutionaries, but successful businessmen and women. Li Shufu, the boss of Chinese carmakers Geely, who recently acquired Volvo from Sweden is there; co-starring with him on the wall of fame are Ren Zhengfei,

who set up Huawei, the telecommunications giant, and, most famous of all, the mercurial Jack Ma, founder of online retailer Alibaba. Homage is also paid to the first Chinese merchant, Fan Li, who some 2,500 years ago traded in Zhejiang province, and to a fellow Zhejiang resident born in the ninth century, Li Linde, the first known Chinese merchant to trade with Japan. Zhejiang province has neither natural resources nor good quality farmland, so its ingenious inhabitants have found other ways to scratch a living.

Where Zhejiang province led, others followed. Figures about China's growth are astonishing.

Around 600 million people have been lifted out of
dire poverty; there are some 60 million successful
private businesses registered, including some of
the world's biggest Internet companies. Jack Ma's
company, Alibaba, sells more than e-Bay and
Amazon combined. China has two hundred, or more,
billionaires, and McKinsey, the global consultancy
firm, estimates that by
2020 the percentage
of urban households
with annual incomes of
between US $15,000
and US $33,000 will
have grown from
8 percent in 2010 to
59 percent. As the
ratio of urban to rural
households has now
passed 51 percent that
means an even greater
increase in the newly
emerging middle class.
Nevertheless, doing
business in China is still
hard. The World Bank's
Doing Business report for
2015, on the ease or otherwise of trading
with China, ranks it an underwhelming 90th out
of 189 economies.

Furthermore, political interference in business is
still a fact of life. Article 19 of China's company law
states that a Party cell must be set up in every firm
above a certain size, whether it is public or private.

Professor William Kirby of Harvard Business School summarizes the "China miracle" as the Chinese people "opening their doors and finding other means to economic prosperity, by working around the barriers posed by the Party."

President Xi Jinping's government has moved away from state investment in infrastructure toward growth driven by consumption and the service sector. According to the *Economist*'s China correspondent, state controlled banks are now being encouraged to help private sector companies, after years of making it hard for them to raise finance; and between 2010 and 2013, the private sector received over half of all loans made by China's banks, up by 25 percent since 2009.

THE NEXT DECADE

Investment in infrastructure may be down, but the service sector is growing in leaps and bounds: from education to entertainment, from health care to hairdressing, the rising middle classes expect more and better, and both foreign and domestic firms are moving in to this market. According to the UK-based Institute of Export, consumers are "gradually shifting from luxury brand-led purchases to choices based on product quality, unique designs, individualism, leisure experience, and personal benefits." This shift has led to new business opportunities; among those listed on the Web site of the China–Britain Business Council are Chinese companies looking to import high-quality, safe products that their consumers can trust in the fields of baby food, biscuits, beauty products, and many more, as well as Chinese firms seeking partnerships with overseas companies in areas ranging from music production to sports tourism.

BUSINESS PROTOCOL

The Chinese who deal with foreigners are well aware of China's attraction for potential business partners and are very knowledgeable about technology, pricing, and world markets. Everything will proceed at the pace of the hosts—which can feel very slow. You will not be able to do much to speed things along.

Your Visit

Arrangements for travel within the country will usually be taken care of by the organization you are visiting. You will probably be met by representatives of the organization when you arrive and seen off by them when you leave and they will look after you well.

Seniority Matters

The Chinese are status conscious, and in more traditional (usually state-run) organizations, when you are meeting a group of people, the most senior figure will often be introduced first. He or she may have an honorific but vague title such as President. However, the actual person with whom you proceed to negotiate may well be younger and probably more at ease with overseas visitors. It is important (though not always easy) to clarify just who is in charge. Your interpreter/fixer should be able to explain how the hierarchy works.

Greeting People

Shake hands with everyone in the group. There is no custom of giving precedence to the female members of the group. The Chinese incline their heads a little on meeting someone new, but there is none of the elaborate bowing that characterizes Japanese culture.

Business Cards

At a business meeting the first thing that happens is an exchange of business cards. When someone hands you a card, make sure to read it, not just glance at it and put it away. It is a good idea to take along a large stock of business cards, with a Chinese version of your name, your company's name, and your job title on the back.

What to Wear

Dress should be formal; for men, suits and ties, with lightweight ones for southern China or for summer in the north. Women can wear trousers, skirts, or suits, but not jeans. Banquets call for more formal wear, so take something extra smart, or go shopping locally—but remember that Chinese clothes sizes may not be right for Western bodies. After years of dressing down, younger Chinese women in particular are enjoying dressing up again; older women (forty plus) tend to dress more soberly and to shun bright colors. Younger Chinese men also often dress colorfully, but until you know your business hosts well, it is better to play it safe.

Time Keeping

Punctuality is considered very important in China, but do not keep looking at your watch, which might imply that you are in a great hurry to finish a deal.

Women in Business

The Chinese are equally happy to deal with both men and women. Women who visit the PRC on business report that they are well accepted by their male Chinese counterparts, and that it is not considered odd if they reciprocate toasts at banquets or take the lead in negotiations.

Virtually everyone has access to e-mail and cell phones, which have revolutionized the possibilities for doing business with China, eliminating the time difference with the USA, Europe, and Australia. E-mail also fits in with the Chinese style of negotiating, allowing time to reflect before responding. Individuals are more empowered now that everyone has their own PC and can correspond directly with business contacts, rather than wading through layers of bureaucracy and relying on bad phone lines.

NEGOTIATING

Presentation

If you prepare well in advance for a meeting in China, it will work better for all concerned. Presentations should be in both Chinese and English, with time allowed for translation. Come with a clear set of objectives, which each side has had time to think about, rather than using the meeting as a brainstorming session.

CHINESE/WESTERN BUSINESS COMMUNICATION STYLES

NAMES
Western: Tend to use first names on first meeting.
Chinese: Use titles such as Mr. or Miss, or Mayor, Manager, Professor.

HUMOR
Western: Tell jokes and use humor as an icebreaker.
Chinese: Little use of humor on first meeting—except for a carefully planned joke.

INTERRUPTIONS
Western: Feel free to interrupt the speaker and put their own point of view, but do not tend to use their phones during a meeting.
Chinese: Interrupting would be rude. Yet people take endless calls on their cell phones! Staff often pop in and whisper messages to senior executives. It is not seen as rude to whisper to a colleague while someone else is speaking.

MAKING SURE YOU ARE UNDERSTOOD
Western: It is usual to structure presentations and to recap what has been said. It is normal for the audience to ask for clarification if necessary. The speaker is to blame if something is not as clear as it should be.
Chinese: Being clearly understood is not a priority, perhaps because saying "I don't understand" is a possible loss of face, and because vagueness may be safer than being specific.

ARGUMENT VS. AGREEMENT
Western: People expect to argue things through; it is not rude to be adversarial.
Chinese: The Chinese are argumentative among themselves, but close ranks in front of a foreigner.

ATTENTION SPAN

Western: Short, and getting shorter. Westerners assume that people will be bored and try to come to the point quickly.

Chinese: Longer. The Chinese are trained from early childhood to listen politely and patiently. They do not come to the point quickly and you may not hear the information you have been waiting for until the meeting is almost over.

EYE CONTACT

Western: Too much eye contact makes people uneasy. Too little and they distrust you.

Chinese: Keep eye contact with your interlocutor. People who avoid eye contact are not considered trustworthy.

PRAISE

Western: Politeness and praise are important, but too much is seen as flattery and is mistrusted.

Chinese: Flattery is part of the negotiating process. It is given by praising people in front of their peers, and by expressing deference to superiors.

SELF DEPRECATION

Western: Used frequently in Britain, less so in the USA.

Chinese: Individuals rarely criticize themselves, but may criticize their organization, or China. This is often used as a gambit, to make themselves seem weaker.

GETTING THINGS DONE

Western: Orders and instructions are direct. They can be questioned.

Chinese: Orders are given more indirectly, but compliance is expected. Instructions are vague, yet carry authority.

When "No" Means "Maybe"

A Chinese person may feel that a direct "no" to a request would be embarrassing and may try to convey disagreement by evading the question or laughing. He or she may have to consult their superiors, or extract certain concessions from you before answering. Quiet persistence and patience is the best way to play this.

Bribery

Requests for "commissions" (that is, bribes) are sadly common, but are likely to be made indirectly. Bribery is a dangerous game to get into and may not help your cause anyway, as the Chinese government is in the midst of a sweeping anti-corruption campaign. As well as arresting thousands of Chinese officials and business people for corruption, it is making an example of foreign companies, such as GSK, the pharmaceuticals company accused of paying bribes to get business.

Outcomes

Westerners tend to expect results from meetings. Chinese meetings, however, are an opportunity for people to state a negotiating position decided in advance. There is rarely a written agenda (though hidden ones are common). There is a strict observance of rank as to who does the talking, and interrupting is considered rude. In more modern, go-ahead companies meetings will be less formal, with more of the lively give and take that Westerners are used to.

Final Decisions Are Not Final

It can take a long time for a contract to be signed. The Chinese side may request changes to a contract even after it has been signed; get it translated into Chinese to speed things up. Remember, long-term relationships are considered more important than quick deals.

Help is at Hand

There are many sources of help for businesses that want to set up in China. There are government-sponsored business promotion bodies in most countries, often with offices in China. Chinese organizations may have a good Web site, but do not neglect to conduct due diligence before trusting them. There are thousands of Web sites and books about doing business in China, some listed at the back of this one.

ENTERTAINING: THE BANQUET

While almost every facet of life has changed in China over the last two decades, the style of a traditional banquet has altered little, though the anti-corruption campaign means less money is spent on them. Whether you are working, studying, or even just holidaying in China, you are likely to be entertained in this way at least once; if you are hoping to do business there, you will have to reciprocate.

The Good Guest

The timeslot for a banquet is usually from 6:30 a.m. to 8:30 p.m. Dress smartly; behavior will be surprisingly formal. Conversation will often be just between the most senior member of the

Chinese organization and his or her counterpart on the Western side. Everyone else, more junior in rank, will tend to eat in silence, despite the Western visitor's well-meaning attempts to get them to chat. This is most marked at banquets with senior politicians, where sometimes the minister will do all the talking, while his retinue limit themselves to showing their appreciation of the conversation (or monologue).

Greetings
Shake hands with everyone, in order of rank; this will be the order in which they are introduced. Exchange cards with people you have not met, using both hands to present your card. If you have brought gifts, leave the giving of them to the end of the meal.

Seating and Table Arrangements
The Chinese host, who usually sits facing the door, will place the most eminent guest in the seat of honor to his right, and the deputy Chinese host will place the next most senior guest on his or her right, at the opposite side of the table. The interpreter will probably sit to the right of the most important guest, with hosts and guests seated alternately around the table.

Be prepared to use chopsticks, though you can request a knife and fork. Most foreigners manage to persuade chopsticks to convey some food to their mouths; few master the knack of holding them properly, which Chinese children learn at their mother's knee. Asking for a demonstration from your hosts can be a good ice-breaker and cause much laughter.

Pace Yourself

Banquets can consist of up to a dozen courses, so pace yourself. Taste a little of every dish or you will never make it to the end of the meal. The author once went to a wonderful banquet, laid on by the conductor of the Shanghai Orchestra, to welcome the Berlin Philharmonic to China, the first such visit made by Western musicians after the Cultural Revolution ended. There were no fewer than forty-two courses, all produced from a kitchen about one meter square.

Do not be surprised if your host is continually placing the tastiest morsels on your plate—this is one way of honoring a guest, who should always wait to be urged to eat before helping himself. Watch what the Chinese diners do when they help themselves to the communal dish of food—they may use a serving spoon, or their own chopsticks. There may also be "public chopsticks" (*gong kuai*) used by everyone to serve themselves.

Lifting your bowl of soup or rice close to your mouth is not rude, and makes eating soup and rice less hazardous. There is a Chinese saying that after a good meal the tablecloth should look like a battlefield—so if you have made a mess of the area around your bowl, do not worry.

The Chinese do not, as a rule, eat dessert, although fresh fruit may be provided. If there is any rice, it will be served near the end of the meal: it is seen as a "filler," in case guests are still hungry, and therefore it is polite to leave some in your bowl to show you have been well fed.

Toasts and Tea

Alcohol is used for toasts, but few Chinese are heavy
drinkers. You will probably find three glasses beside
your plate, one for beer, one for wine, and one for a
more fiery liquor, *maotai*, or *baijiu* (white liquor),
which is distilled from sorghum and is up to
65 percent proof. *Maotai* is usually used for toasts,
and you will often see the Chinese finish off a whole
glass each time (but they are very small glasses).

Green tea may also be served and it is perfectly
alright to ask for tea, just as it is not rude to avoid
alcohol if that is what you want to do. Vegetarians
may have a harder time of things than teetotallers;
if you are vegetarian, warn your hosts in advance.
If you only eat halal or kosher food, you may be
out of luck, despite the history of Moslem influence
in China; however, there are restaurants in most
cities run by people from Xinjiang province, so
that might offer a solution.

Making Speeches and Proposing Toasts

Speeches, which end with one side toasting the
other, usually take place soon after the beginning
of the meal. The host will probably speak between
the arrival of the first and second dishes, and the
chief guest should reply a few minutes later, after
the start of the second dish. Keep your speech
short and bland and follow it with a toast. Make a
few appreciative comments about your visit, add
some remarks about hopes for future cooperation,
and avoid elaborate jokes as they are often
untranslatable.

Beware Jokes!
A Canadian journalist writes of how he was once at a banquet in the Great Hall of the People in Beijing. During the speeches, a visiting diplomat embarked upon a long and complicated joke in English. The poor Chinese interpreter, having tried in vain to translate it, finally despaired. He simply said, in Chinese, "The honored foreign visitor has just told a joke— please laugh!" The audience obliged.

Cheers!
At the end of the toast, the proposer says "*ganbei*" (literally, "dry glasses"), but caution is advisable because there will often be a number of toasts to follow. All-purpose "safe" toasts such as "To the friendship between our countries/companies/schools," are the order of the day, and normally people do not clink their glasses together. Guests may eventually propose slightly more original toasts, especially once they have downed a few glasses of *maotai*. The consumption of large amounts of very expensive alcohol at banquets is being officially discouraged as part of the ongoing anti-corruption drive.

Making Conversation
Food and sport are good topics of conversation. Avoid talking about religion, bureaucracy, politics, sex, Tibet, or Taiwan. Other safe topics include families, holidays, tourism, travel, and, of course, your business.

THE RETURN MATCH

If you decide to arrange a return banquet for your Chinese hosts before you leave, ask your interpreter, or whoever is organizing your visit, to help you. A table plan should be drawn up, and at a very formal banquet there should be place cards. As host it will be your job to keep plying your guests with food, and other people in your organization can do likewise to the person seated near them, especially each time a new dish arrives. Your guests will decline something offered to them several times before they feel able to accept, so you will have to keep pressing them to eat. It is hard work being the host or a guest at a Chinese banquet, but they can be rewarding nonetheless.

A Change of Style

When American President George W. Bush went to Beijing, Western rather than Chinese food was served at the welcoming banquet. As the banquet drew to a close, in place of the usual hasty farewells, an accordionist materialized on stage, and Bush's host, President Jiang Zemin, serenaded the Americans with a rendering of "O sole mio"!

WORKING IN CHINA

There are increasing numbers of foreigners working in China, in teaching, business, the media, science, and in the newer private sector companies. Advice on how to find a job, getting the correct type of visa (*very* important), writing a suitable CV, checking (and amending if need be) your employment contract, and finding a place to live is available online. Unless you work directly for a foreign company such as a bank or an international organization, you will not earn a fortune from working in China, but you can save quite a lot of your salary and you will have an experience you will never forget. You will make the move from a transient tourist, just there to have fun (and go shopping), to the privileged position of someone who can become a part of Chinese life. Plus you will have the chance to travel, learn Chinese, make lifelong friends—and you can still go shopping!

chapter nine

COMMUNICATING

MANDARIN, CANTONESE, AND MORE

China's mountains and deserts have always made communications difficult, so it is not surprising that different forms of the language have developed. These are often referred to as "dialects," but since they are often mutually unintelligible, they may be thought of as separate languages. There are eight major variants of the Chinese language, including Mandarin, Cantonese, Shanghainese, Hakka, Amoy, Fuzhou, and Wenzhou, as well as minor regional variations. Mandarin is the official language used in both the PRC and Taiwan as the medium of education, and is the common means of communication in China. In the PRC it is called *putonghua* (common or standard speech), as well as *hanyu* (the language of the Han people) and *zhongwen* (Chinese). In Taiwan it is known as *guoyu* or *huayu* (national language).

Chinese is a tonal language, part of the Sino-Tibetan family of languages. English, by contrast, belongs to the Indo-European family. There are other South Asian languages that work in the same way as Chinese: Vietnamese, Burmese, and Thai, for example. Tonal languages are those in which a variation in the pitch of the voice conveys differences in meaning. For example, *tang* said in a high, level tone means "soup," but *tang* said in a rising tone means "sugar"; *gou* said in a fall-rise tone means "dog," but *gou* said with a falling tone means "enough." There are four tones in Mandarin. Cantonese has six. The four tones are:

level

rising

fall-rise

falling

Most Chinese words are made up of one syllable, each represented by a single Chinese character. Chinese has fewer sounds than some other languages; as English has more sounds, there are few actual Chinese sounds (as opposed to tones) that pose problems for English speakers. Foreigners have trouble even *hearing* the different tones, never mind reproducing them. If you ask your Chinese contacts to help you improve your pronunciation, you still won't get it right, but your hosts can have a lot of fun helping you. Any minor difficulty you may have in learning some simple phrases will be far outweighed by the positive reaction you will get from Chinese people, and the context, as well as the willingness of your hosts to respond to your efforts, will help understanding.

The Standard of English in China
The standard of spoken English in the cities is improving all the time; it is better taught, there are more native English speakers working in China, people travel more and there is (almost) unlimited access to English-language films, Web sites, books, and music. Plus, the motivation for learning English is greater than ever.

In the countryside, few will know English or any other foreign language; rural schools have trouble recruiting and retaining teachers who can teach anything other than very basic subjects. When using English with people who do not speak it, use short sentences, speak slowly, and try not to use unnecessarily difficult words, or slang. If you are using an interpreter, try not to say too much at a time—give him or her a chance to interpret a manageable amount before you move on to the next sentence.

Some Chinese, especially Cantonese speakers, tend to stress all English syllables equally, leading to a sort of machine-gun effect; combined with the fact that "please," "thank you," and "sorry" are not used nearly as often in Chinese, this may lead to a perception of rudeness.

Pidgin English

The word "pidgin" (pronounced "pigeon," like the bird) comes from early Chinese attempts to pronounce the word "business." When traders from other countries first visited the coasts of China in the early 1800s they had no shared language. Pidgin English, consisting of a few hundred useful English words, filled this linguistic vacuum. The blend was enriched by a smattering of Hindi, brought over by traders from the East India Company. After 1949 pidgin died out; until then it was used as a way for foreigners and Chinese to communicate, as well as by speakers of different Chinese dialects to talk to each other.

Picturesque words from those days survive in stories such as *Tin Tin*, words like "*chop chop*," meaning hurry up. "*Chop*" on its own meant a trademark, or a name stamp on a contract. Another favorite is "*joss*" (as in joss-stick, a stick of incense),which comes from the Portuguese word *deos* (God); from this came the wonderful "*joss-pidgin-man,*" or "God business man"— better known as a priest.

BODY LANGUAGE

Unlike in some of the more traditional societies in Southeast Asia, the visitor to China does not have to negotiate a minefield of possible ways of offending their host. Years of compulsorily identifying with the "workers, peasants, and soldiers" (that is, the poorest classes of society) have made the Chinese relatively relaxed about body language. So long as you display ordinary good manners, that will be perfectly acceptable.

One thing you are less likely to see than in Europe, and which you should not initiate, is kissing in public; hugging and other exuberant "touchy-feely" Western body language is still uncommon. Among the educated urban young, and especially among fans of American movies, this is changing, however, and hugging, kissing, shouting with happiness, and other normal ways that young people in the West behave are growing, as the young shed the protective layers of inhibition their parents' generation built up over the years.

CHINESE CHARACTERS

Chinese is among the world's oldest written languages. It has no alphabet, but instead has around 50,000 characters. Many characters go back as far as the

Shang dynasty, around 1500 BCE. Early Chinese writing was based on pictograms, which evolved into characters formed by a series of brushstrokes. Some characters still resemble pictograms: for example, the sun (*taiyang*) was a once a circle with a dot in the middle; now it is written like a box with a line across it. Water (*shui*) is three flowing lines; a person (*ren*) looks like a little headless human with two legs. Two characters can be combined to make a new one: "sun" plus "moon" make the character for "bright." The character for "family" is formed by putting "roof" over "pig" (because rural families kept pigs, not because everyone disliked their family members).

Most characters consist of two parts: the radical, which shows to which class the word belongs, and the phonetic, which tells how it is pronounced. For example, the character for pure, or clear, *qing*, has two parts; the water radical and the part which gives the pronunciation, *qing*. There are about 250 radicals, some quite common, such as the one used for anything concerned with fire, others more unusual. Although learning characters appears a nightmarish task to Westerners, Chinese children start young and work hard at it. The literacy rate

清　氵

water radical
(word category)

青

phonetic element
(pronunciation)

is 96.4 percent (UNESCO, 2015) and a functional knowledge of between three and four thousand characters is enough for most people.

PINYIN, OR HOW TO ROMANIZE CHINESE CHARACTERS

The modern system of transliteration, Pinyin, was developed by the PRC in the 1950s, replacing the older Wade–Giles system. It can be confusing to read books written some years ago with differently Romanized versions of Chinese place-names, such as Soochow, now written Suzhou.

Pinyin is invaluable: telephone directories and dictionaries use it, and since Chinese does not have an alphabet, this is the only way to organize information. Keypads use Pinyin: if you type in the word *ma*, using the two letters *m* and *a*, the screen gives you a choice of the different Chinese characters used to write the word, depending on its meaning (*ma* can mean mother, horse, and other things, depending on its tone and how it is written). You then choose the correct character.

Signs in public spaces are often in Pinyin and in English—even so, knowledge of at least a few Chinese characters is useful (exit, entrance, and so on), but not as vital as knowledge of the spoken language.

THE SOUNDS OF PINYIN.

Here is a written guide to the sounds of Pinyin; there are many apps that you can download to help you pronounce Chinese words correctly.

- **c** is pronounced as *ts* in "cats"
- **z** is pronounced as *ds* in "seeds"
- **q** is pronounced as *ch* in "cheap"
- **j** is pronounced as *j* in "jig"
- **x** is pronounced as something between *sh* in "shin" and *s*
- **s** as in "siesta"
- **r** is pronounced as a cross between *s* in "vision" and *r* in "red"
- **h** is pronounced as *ch* in Scottish "loch"
- **zh** is pronounced as *j* in "July"
- **a** is like *ar* in "far"
- **-ang** is like *ung* in Southern English "sung"
- **e** is like *er* in "her"
- **en** is like *en* in "stricken"
- **ei** is like *ay* in "hay"
- **ou** is like *ou* in "soul"
- **i** is like *ee* in "see," except after c,s,z,r, ch,sh, and zh, when it is like the *i* in American "sir"
- **u** is like *oo* in "soon"
- **Ï** is like *e* in "see" but said with the lips rounded as if for "oo"
- **-ong** is like *ung* in German "Jung"
- **-ian** is like "yen"
- **ui** is like "way"

THE MEDIA
Censorship
All media in China are state controlled, and the Orwellian sounding SARFT (State Administration of Radio, Film, and Television) checks programs before broadcast. Journalists are often self-censoring for their own survival. Hard-hitting interviews with politicians are rare; news and current affairs broadcasts are prerecorded, rather than live, or with a ten-second delay. The French organization Reporters without Borders ranks China very low down (168 out of 178) on its annual media freedom index.

Foreign broadcasters such as CNN often have to pass their signal through a Chinese controlled satellite, so content can be blacked out quickly if they mention certain key phrases, such as the Dalai Lama, or the poisoned baby milk scandal of 2008. However the Internet allows people much more freedom to watch and listen to what they want, and satellite signal hacking systems can be bought for around 2,000 RMB (US $285) to access channels otherwise unobtainable.

TV and Radio
There are about 3,000 TV channels in China, and many local and national radio stations, some state run, some private, many available only online. TV and radio also broadcast in minority languages, such as Tibetan or Uyghur. CCTV is the state broadcaster, with foreign-language TV channels as well as 45 Chinese TV channels showing news, drama, music, and so on. TV used to have enormous audiences, but, just as in the West, these are fragmenting as there are so many other sources of entertainment.

Print

China has two main state controlled news agencies, Xinhua and the China News Service. *Renmin Ribao* (*People's Daily*) is the government's official newspaper. Its English-language sister paper is *China Daily*, published in a print and an online version. Altogether, there are over 2,000 newspapers and 7,000 magazines, some state owned, many private, up from a mere forty-two in 1968—all Communist Party papers. In addition, around 25,000 printing houses and bookstores print and sell everything from educational material, pirated translations of *Harry Potter*, and American business guides to romances, pornography, detective fiction, and specialist journals. Books are cheap and many Chinese are avid readers. Bookshops such as the huge one on Wanfujing, Beijing's main shopping street, are crammed not only with books, but also with customers of all ages, from children who can barely toddle to newly retired workers hungry for self-improvement.

SOCIAL MEDIA

Internet speeds in China are often faster than in Western countries, the devices used are newer and cheaper, and young Chinese in particular have adopted social media with enthusiasm, for work, dating, shopping, planning nights out, booking tickets, and so on. We Chat is a messaging app, QQ is similar to Facebook, and Weibo is the Chinese equivalent of Twitter. Around 3,000 Western Internet sites are blocked—Google, Facebook, and YouTube among them.

Social media have had a huge impact on every aspect of life in China, not least on news reporting. For example, in July 2011 two high-speed trains collided near Wenzhou in Zhejiang province. Four railway carriages fell from the high-speed viaduct, forty people died, and over a hundred were injured. In the West this would have been front-page news. But local officials panicked, brought the rescue operations to a premature conclusion, and ordered the railway carriages to be buried. However, "burying bad news" is a harder act to pull off now than in pre-Internet days. The online community found out what had happened and there was public outrage, at which point the normally cautious official media had to cover the story—a small victory for "citizen journalists."

TELEPHONE

When China first opened up to the world, it was quicker to take a taxi across town to talk to someone than to get through to them on the telephone. The residents of an entire apartment block might share one very poor quality phone line between them. As phones were used by so many people, they were thought to harbor germs, so people often covered the receiver with a handkerchief, making it even harder to hear what they were saying. At work, people tended to use the office phone to make all the calls they couldn't make from home—so no one could ever get through to workplaces either. Telephone directories were almost

unknown, due to the obsession with secrecy: foreign embassies often had one, but kept it under lock and key. Now the Chinese are making up for lost time by talking incessantly everywhere they go on the latest smartphones. Buy a Chinese SIM card and maybe a new Chinese-made phone when you arrive; it will be invaluable.

MAIL
China Post's green and yellow post offices and delivery vans can be seen everywhere. Sending parcels and letters by surface mail takes time (a month from China to the UK is not unusual) but is cheap and reliable; airmail is quicker of course. Internet deliveries in China often use China Post, and have given the service a new lease of life.

CONCLUSION
The contradictions inherent in the Chinese pursuit of Western-style economic prosperity combined with tight political control were highlighted by former US Secretary of Treasury Henry Paulson in 2015, when he said: "It seems . . . incongruous to be, on the one

hand, so committed to fostering more competition and market-driven flexibility in the economy, yet on the other hand, to be seeking more control in the political sphere, the media, and the Internet." These contradictions have not stopped China's economic growth powering the world economy for the past three decades, but now that it is slowing down, they may come home to roost. Mountains of unacknowledged debt may never be repaid and structural reforms and more transparency are urgently needed. Caught in the middle of the transition from a state-controlled, investment-led economy to a market-led one driven by the private sector are the ordinary Chinese, who, although they enjoy life more, constantly fear being left behind. Shanghai based writer, Mao Jian, describes the pressure felt by people governed by a new concept of "Chinese Time": "Got to speed up to make a buck. Tear down the old courtyard, fill in Suzhou Creek, register that domain name. One day late is forever late. Longevity is no longer the goal; speed is the style in China today."

Where earlier generations were brought up to "Serve the People," and urged to imitate romanticized revolutionary heroes such as the penniless but perfect soldier and gentleman Lei Feng, nowadays China's role models are both real and rich. Foreign entrepreneurs such as Apple's founder Steve Jobs, and home grown ones like the diminutive Jack Ma (he stands five foot tall), creator of the Internet giant Alibaba, are admired and imitated. Yet striving to succeed has arguably always been part of the Chinese character: many seem to be born entrepreneurs, willing to take risks, who work hard, save hard, and dream of getting rich. As the government retreats from managing its citizens' everyday lives, people are simply continuing the old traditions of relying on their own efforts and on strong family ties, combined with a new awareness of the wider world.

China's rulers run a tight ship, and foreign visitors should never underestimate the all-encompassing powers of what remains an authoritarian and sometimes unpredictable regime. You as a "foreign friend" may be simply there to marvel at the story so far, or privileged enough to play a part in the next chapter of the Chinese story. But over the thirty years that the writer of this book has been lucky enough to know the country, Chinese friends, colleagues, and students have continued to combine a mixture of warmth, loyalty, a ready sense of humor, a belief in the value of hard work, and a pride in their country's achievements, tempered with realism and the knowledge that there is still much to do. As UK-based Sinologist Martin Jaques puts it: "While possessed of the kind of inner confidence and experience that comes from being the heirs of a great civilization, the Chinese have no illusions about where they have got to and the tasks that lie ahead." All the experts predict that China will have an even greater influence on the twenty-first century than it had on the twentieth; which is why time spent getting to know this fascinating country and its people will be an investment for life.

Appendix: Simple Vocabulary

Ni hao?
Hello (lit., you good?)

Zaijian
Goodbye (lit., again see)

Xie xie
Thank you

Bu keqi
You're welcome
(in reply to thank you)

Duibuqi
Sorry, excuse me (not used as
much as in English)

Duile
Yes (lit., correct)

Shi de
Yes (lit., it is so)

Bu shi
No (lit., it is not so)

Qing zuo
Please be seated

Qing gei wo
Please give me

Qing jin
Please come in

Yingguo
England

Yingyu
English (language)

Meiguo
America

Zhongguo
China

Zhonguoren
Chinese man/woman

Hanyu (in the PRC)
Chinese (language)

Jianada
Canada

Aodaliya
Australia

Wo bu hui shuo hanyu
I can't speak Chinese

Wo shi
I am . . .

Zai nar
Where is . . .?

Canguan
Restaurant

Jiudian
Hotel

Cesuo
Toilet

Huochezhan
Railway station

Feijizhan
Airport

Note: There are no direct equivalents for "Yes," "No," or "Please."
For "Yes" you could use *duile*, which really means "correct," or you
can say *shi de*, which means "it is so." Instead of "No" you could
sometimes use *bu shi*.

Further Reading

For analysis of all aspects of life in China, *The Economist* is excellent and the *China Daily* is worth reading. There are thousands of books on business, travel, sociology, history, and more, and much good fiction, too, as well as thousands of specialized Web sites and blogs. The following list is a tiny microcosm of what is available.

Chang, Jung. *Wild Swans: Three Daughters of China*. London: Flamingo (Harper Collins), 1993.

Chang, Jung and John Halliday. *Mao: The Unknown Story*. London: Jonathan Cape, 2005.

Fenby, Jonathan. *The Penguin History of Modern China, The Fall and Rise of a Great Power*. London: Penguin, 2008.

Harney, Alexandra. *The China Price: The True Cost of Chinese Competitive Advantage*. New York: Penguin Press, 2008.

Hessler, Peter. *Oracle Bones: A Journey Through Time in China*. New York: Harper Perennial, 2007.

Hong Fincher, Leta. *Leftover Women: The Resurgence of Gender Inequality in China*. London: Zed Books, 2014.

Kissinger, Henry. *On China*. New York: Penguin Press, reprinted 2012.

McGregor, James. *One Billion Customers: Lessons from the Front Lines of Doing Business in China*. New York: Simon and Schuster, 2005.

Min, Anchee. *Red Azalea*. New York: Random House, 1994.

Min, Anchee. *Empress Orchid*. London: Bloomsbury, 2004.

Qiu, Xiaolong. *Death of a Red Heroine*. New York: Soho Press, 2000.

Qiu, Xiaolong. *The Mao Case*. New York: Minotaur Books, 2009.

Xinran. *The Good Women Of China, Hidden Voices*. London: Vintage, 2003.

Xinran. *Message from an Unknown Chinese Mother: Stories of Loss and Love*. London: Vintage, 2011.

Torrens, Christopher. *Doing Business in China*. London: Economist Books, 2010.

Web Sites, Search Engines, and Apps

There are countless Web sites devoted to every aspect of life in China written by Western journalists, bloggers, foodies, travelers, and wannabes of every shade. Many more are set up by the Chinese themselves, some in English as well as in Chinese. The following list is a tiny sample of what is out there, which the author of this book has found useful and interesting.

Popular Chinese Web Sites

Baidu is the most popular search engine in China, and you can also use it to download TV shows, music, and films. Copyright concerns do not appear to bother it overmuch.

QQ is an instant messaging service and offers a service similar to Facebook as well as news and music, shopping and games. Its star is waning, though, and Ten Cent is taking over.

Sina.com is a government run news site.

Weibo is the Chinese answer to Twitter. Many users "follow" Chinese celebrities on Weibo.

Taobao is the Chinese equivalent to Amazon, online shopping heaven. JD.com is also considered good, for genuine as opposed to counterfeit products. Amazon has become more popular since introducing a pay-on-delivery service.

Youku This is the equivalent of YouTube for China, used for watching music videos , TV shows, and so on.

Ctrip is very useful for booking flights, hotels, and trips to sights such as the Great Wall or the Terracotta Warriors. It is available in many languages as well as English and Chinese.

Other Web Sites and Apps

Chinadialogue.net An independent and widely respected source of news and topical discussion about politics, the environment, and society in China today. The site is bilingual.

The online sites of the BBC, the *Economist*, and many other quality newspapers carry an enormous amount of information about China's political and economic scene. The Chinese government-run newspaper *China Daily* has a useful site, though it is of course censored.

The BBC also produces free online Chinese language lessons, as does CCTV (China Central TV) and many others. There are online forums that discuss the most (and least) useful sites and materials for learning Chinese.

There are so many expat blogs now about the joys and problems of life in China that the best way to find one that suits you is to look at the Expats. Blog.com directory of China blogs.

Journalistsresource.org is a not-for-profit online resource (written by Harvard University in the USA), which has many useful articles on aspects of life in China such as science and technology research, population, the environment, urban growth, and growing income disparities.

culture smart! china

Index

Acknowledgments

I would like to dedicate this book to all my dear friends in China who made me so welcome in the 1980s, and to my Chinese students in the UK, who have taught me far more than I taught them.